ALL ANYBODY NEEDS TO KNOW
ABOUT INDEPENDENT CONTRACTING

Connie Wright-Nicolette

ALL ANYBODY NEEDS TO KNOW ABOUT INDEPENDENT CONTRACTING

With Forms, Instructions and Other Helpful Items

Shelly Waxman, J.D.

Writers Club Press
New York Lincoln Shanghai

ALL Anybody Needs to Know About Independent Contracting
With Forms, Instructions and Other Helpful Items

All Rights Reserved © 2003 by Sheldon R. Waxman

No part of this book may be reproduced or transmitted in any form or by any means, graphic, electronic, or mechanical, including photocopying, recording, taping, or by any information storage retrieval system, without the written permission of the publisher.

Writers Club Press
an imprint of iUniverse, Inc.

For information address:
iUniverse
2021 Pine Lake Road, Suite 100
Lincoln, NE 68512
www.iuniverse.com

ISBN: 0-595-26272-4

Printed in the United States of America

CONTENTS

ACKNOWLEDGEMENTS ix
PREFACE xi

PART I
INTRODUCTION

CHAPTER 1
DEFINITIONS 3
CHAPTER 2
THE MASTER-SLAVE RELATIONSHIP 5
CHAPTER 3
A BUSINESS OF ONE 7
CHAPTER 4
THE BIRTH OF THE SAFE HARBOR TEST—A VICTORY
    FOR THE AMERICAN PEOPLE 12

PART II
FOR INDIVIDUALS

CHAPTER 5
WHY BE AN INDEPENDENT CONTRACTOR 23
CHAPTER 6
REQUIREMENTS FOR IC STATUS 28

PART III
FOR COMPANIES

CHAPTER 7
WHY IT IS A NECESSITY FOR YOUR BUSINESS TO USE
  INDEPENDENT CONTRACTORS 35

CHAPTER 8
RESISTANCE TO CHANGE CAUSES TRADITIONAL
  ADVISORS NEGATIVITY 37

CHAPTER 9
A BUSINESSMAN'S PERSPECTIVE 39

CHAPTER 10
CONVERSIONS 43

CHAPTER 11
ACCOUNTING AND TAX SAVING TIPS FOR THE SERVICE
  PROVIDER AND SERVICE RECIPIENT 45

CHAPTER 12
REQUIREMENTS FOR INDEPENDENT CONTRACTOR
  TREATMENT 49

PART IV
FOR CORPORATE OFFICERS

CHAPTER 13
DUAL HAT STATUS 53

CHAPTER 14
PROTOCOLS FOR SETTING UP YOUR OWN BUSINESS
  UNDER THE "TWO HAT SYSTEM" 56

CHAPTER 15
REQUIREMENTS FOR INDEPENDENT CONTRACTOR
  STATUS 59

APPENDIX
PART V
FORMS, INSTRUCTIONS AND OTHER HELPFUL ITEMS

CHAPTER 16
LAW 63
CHAPTER 17
BIBLIOGRAPHY AND WEBSITES 66
CHAPTER 18
FORMS, INSTRUCTIONS AND WORKSHEETS 68
CHAPTER 19
VARIOUS AGREEMENTS AND OPTIONAL CLAUSES 76
  FloA's General Independent Contractor Agreement 76
  Independent Contractor Agreement for Household Workers 82
  Independent Contractor Agreement for Real Estate Salesperson 87
  Independent Contractor Agreement for Construction Contractor 94
  Independent Contractor Agreement for Creative Contractor 100
  Independent Contractor Agreement for General Contractor 109
  Independent Contractor Agreement for Accountant & Bookkeeper ..117
  Independent Contractor Agreement for Consultant 123
  Independent Contractor Agreement for Direct Seller 132
  Independent Contractor Agreement for Work Made for Hire 138
  Contract Amendment Form 147
  Additional Agreement Clauses 148
CHAPTER 20
THE IRS IS ON OUR SIDE 155
CHAPTER 21
AUTHOR'S BIOGRAPHY 233

ACKNOWLEDGEMENTS

This book is dedicated to my Mom (who has overcome some terrible hardships and survives), Dad (gone but never forgotten), Josiah (my lovable bright son), Zoe (my adorable smart daughter), Kathy (my wife), Rich (the businessman in Chapter 4), all my other good friends and to all those trying to free themselves from the wage slave employment system.

"The natural liberty of man is to be free from any superior power on earth, and not to be under the will or legislative authority of man, but to have only the law of nature for his rule." John Locke

"If a man empties his purse into his head no one can take it away from him. An investment in knowledge always pays the best interest." Benjamin Franklin

Other Books by Author: "In the Teeth of The Wind—A Study of Power and How to Fight It." (2002). Available at www.thelawyer.info

PREFACE

A MAJOR goal for everybody should be to free oneself from the EMPLOYMENT TRAP. We urge you to explore this subject and make it your personal goal to become an INDEPENDENT CONTRACTOR yourself or to hire INDEPENDENT CONTRACTORS.

The following is what some very savvy people say about independent contracting:

SAM WALTON: "I've made it my own personal mission to ensure that constant change is a vital part of the Wal-Mart culture itself. I've forced change—sometimes for change's sake alone—at every turn in our company's development. In fact, I think one of the greatest strengths of Wal-Mart's ingrained culture is its ability to drop everything and turn on a dime."

"You start with a given: free enterprise is the engine of our society; communism is pretty much down the drain and proven so; and there doesn't appear t be anything else that can compare to a free society based on a market economy. Nothing can touch that system. We can do it better than the Japanese because we're more innovative, we're more creative. We can compete with labor in Bangladesh or wherever because we have better technology, which can give us more efficient equipment. We can get beyond a lot of our old adversarial relationships and establish win-win partnerships with our suppliers and our workers, which will leave us with more energy and talent to focus on the important thing, meeting the needs of our customers. But all this requires overcoming one of the most powerful forces in human nature: the resistance to change. To succeed in this world, you have to change all the time." *Made in America*

PETER DRUCKER: "The possessor of knowledge owns his own 'tools of production' and has the freedom to move to wherever opportunities for effectiveness, for accomplishment and for advancement seem greatest."

"The knowledge society will inevitably become far more competitive than any society we have yet known—for the simple reason that with knowledge being universally accessible, there are no excuses for nonperformance. There will be no 'poor' countries—there will only be ignorant countries. And the same will be true for individual companies, individual industries and individual organizations. It will be true of individuals too." *Managing in a Time of Great Change*

GERRY SPENCE: "The new and most powerful union of all will be a union of one: one man, one woman, one worker with special skills, an inquiring mind, an independent attitude. In the new-age workplace the worker will no longer be a slave. He will enter the place of work voluntarily to do a job for a price, his price. He will leave as he chooses. He will cherish his freedom, which is his security. He cannot be lured into the trap. The master cannot own him."

"The new age worker, belonging to the union of one, has made himself an expert in whatever job he or she undertakes. But he does his work with an expertise that brings order and efficiency to the task. He works to satisfy himself, not the master. Workers will again become independent—and own their own tools. I see it already. The cameraman for network television, an independent contractor, brings his own camera to the news scene, does his work, takes his camera home, and goes scuba diving the rest of the day."

"In the new-age workplace, the engineer, the draftsman, the computer wizard, the designer, every professional and every skilled artisan, yes, a skilled ditch digger as well, can belong to the new union of one. The union dues are free. If the employer does not meet the demands of the union of one, the new-age worker can replace the employer...with a more intelligent, more responsive one; one that better suits the taste and the need of the new-age worker."

"The most valuable worker for the corporation is the worker who no longer demands all of the spangles and sparkles of security that soon soon-dim: the pensions, the benefits that somehow end up enslaving rather than freeing. The old way has become a dismal game in which both master and slave, chained to each other, hate one another, each fighting the other with their respective weapons...The worker, seeking security, like the slave of old, does not seek to do work but to avoid work...The worker's goal is not to live at work but to become embalmed during the working day and to lie in the company's casket until the quitting bell revives him...."

"The worker who seeks security cannot exhibit the free mind necessary to spring ahead on his own. He requires an overseer, a time clock, rules of work, rules of vacations, rules of sick leave, rules about having babies, rules about rules. He requires laws to protect him, and commissions to hear his complaints and representatives to represent him."

"The best employment with the best corporation offering the best life-long security is at best a poor bargain. Get out. Walk out. Run out. Break down the doors but get out..."

"The new-age business will recognize the worker as the source of its wealth, respect the worker, and provide the worker a place of self-discovery and self-expression...."

"The new-age employer and the new-age worker, supported by the new-age union of one will redefine the relationship of worker and employer. The new-age employer will become more of a partner, a supplier of opportunity, an educator, a sharer in dreams, a sharer in profit. The new-age worker will become his own master. He will decide his fate and make and follow his own dreams. He will explore not the master's poisonous caverns of slavery but his own unexplored reaches, in which he will discover his unique self, cherish its value, reject the security of slavery, and encumber his freedom for no one, not even himself." *Seven Simple Steps to Personal Freedom"*

If you have been told that it is too dangerous to be an Independent Contractor or to hire them, DON'T BELIEVE them. It is now easier than ever to be or use Independent Contractors. THE LAW IS ON YOUR SIDE.

This is because of the EXTRAORDINARY litigation in which the IRS was forced to stop turning everybody into an employee. In an edited version this previously untold story is recited in Chapter 4, *infra.* and, also, complete in Chap. 11 of "In the Teeth of the Wind—A Study of Power and How to Fight It." Available at www.thelawyer.info .

I am **available for consultation**, as well as is my organization, Freedom Lawyers of America, experts on the subject of independent contracting and we provide a CERTIFICATION procedure whereby you or your workers are guaranteed to be properly operating as Independent Contractors for IRS and other purposes. E-Mail me at shelly@cybersol.com or shelly@thelawyer.info . This Certification procedure is a FOOL PROOF method of stopping the IRS and other governmental agencies from even attempting a challenge.

SAMPLE

MONEY BACK GUARANTEE

_____, having paid $_____ for our services in providing assistance and our expertise in establishing the proper usage of independent contractors, we guarantee that if it is determined

by a governmental agency that our opinion is erroneous, we will return that sum or credit it against the legal fees necessary to sustain our opinion. This guarantee is conditional to the extent that it applies only to the state of the law as of the date of issuance and for a period of three years therefrom.
Dated:

_____

SAMPLE

CERTIFICATION

_____, having warranted that he will utilize the materials we have provided in the manner we have advised, this is our certification that _____'s use of independent contractors is legally proper and in accordance with IRS Guidelines and we will provide legal assistance and expert testimony to defend _____'s position, if challenged.
Dated:

_____

Of course, you can also do it yourself. That is what this book is for.

PART I

INTRODUCTION

CHAPTER 1

DEFINITIONS

It is hoped that this Book will provide you with the information necessary to attain the Independent Contractor treatment that you are seeking. If there are any questions, please feel free to contact us. To assist in the understanding of what is involved, it is necessary to provide you with the following abbreviations and definitions:

IC=Independent Contractor—a self-employed, independent business person;

SP=Service Provider—You, the Independent Contractor, the one who provides a service to the Service Recipient;

SR=Service Recipient—the person/company who contracts with you (the SP) to do work and provide your services;

ES=Employment status/system—the employment system that depends on the payment of withholding and other taxes and other onerous state and federal regulations, the system you are trying to transform away from;

20CLFT=The 20 common law factor test—which is used by the IRS to determine if you are an IC;

SHT=The Safe Harbor Test—a test, which if you are covered by it will immunize you from any reclassification procedures. The SHT is only available to the companies that hire IC's.

CW=Contingent Workers. This does not include IC's. They are the varying forms of leased or agency workers, who are the outsourced personnel that have become popular with companies. It is not recommended that you become one of these or use these, although some use it as a step in the progression to become an IC. It is not recommended because the SP just becomes a wage slave to the hiring agency and the SR pays a lot to have the agency handle all of the ES regulations, payroll and taxes.

FLoA=Freedom Lawyers of America is an organization which, among other things, provides a foolproof certification procedure, whereby our Independent Contractor Specialists guarantee that you are properly operating as an IC or using IC's for IRS and other purposes. For additional information, see our website: www.thelawyer.info .

CHAPTER 2

THE MASTER-SLAVE RELATIONSHIP

INDEPENDENT CONTRACTORS ARE THE ANSWER

We've turned into a nation of whiners, where employees spend their days hoarding imagined insults and injuries for future lawsuits, and employers are forced to offer continued employment to unsuitable employees. The old adage of an honest day's work for an honest day's pay is no longer valid.

The employer-employee relationship has become an adversarial union based on mutual distrust and suspicion. There used to be an unspoken agreement that was made when you were hired and exchanged a handshake with your new boss. You went to work every day—barring some specific instances—and in return, you received a living wage. I don't know when the time-honored bond between the employed and the employer began to decay, but it seems to have become the norm rather than the exception.

Today's employees expect to start at the top of the business ladder, calling the shots and making the rules, despite their lack of experience, knowledge or skills. Prospective employees now come to the employment table with a list of wants. They don't ask. They demand to receive benefits and considerations that were formerly reserved for trusted longtime employees. Many bring no pertinent skills to the position they're applying for. They want a job but not necessarily work. It might cut into their busy social calendars. Employees have no incentive to develop a sense of company loyalty.

If an employee isn't working out, it almost takes an act of Congress to relieve them of their duties lest the employer be accused of "discrimination." A paper trail of documentation leading back to the dawn of time must now be kept, outlining the employee's transgressions. Even the old "three strikes and you're out" practice no longer applies. Instead of ridding themselves of ill-suited employees, employers must now offer a plethora of professional services to help and rehabilitate the erring employee—over and over and over.

We need a work ethic that allows for mutual respect between employers and employees; one that doesn't break the employer's bank.

CHAPTER 3

A BUSINESS OF ONE

It started around the time the Civil Rights Act of 1964, creating the Equal Employment Opportunity Commission, was passed as part of Lyndon Johnson's Great Society program. Of course the Federal and State Governments had been meddling in the contract between employee and employer long before this with withholding tax requirements, social security, unemployment benefits, workman's compensation, union check off and fair labor standards. But with the creation of the EEOC, personnel practices of private companies became a favorite target of socialistically minded legislators.

It has reached such a stage that the concept of private employment is now a joke. The Federal and State Governments now control employment. Personnel Offices are now called Human Relations Departments—further signifying the encroachment of socialistic concepts. Of course, each State has gotten into the act with their own special brand of legislation. The following are just some of the federal restrictions that have come about since 1964:

a. Pensions-ERISA—Employee Retirement Income Security Act.
b. INS (Immigration and Naturalization Service) regulations.
c. ADEA—Age Discrimination in Employment Act.
d. OSHA—Occupation Safety and Health Act.

Moreover, private causes have action have sprung up, being allowed by the Courts to curtail the right of employers to hire and fire whomever they wanted. This has become a big industry for the legal profession and has spun off a specialty in the law known as employment law.

Will this trend continue? I don't think it can. It has become too costly and too inhuman. People who do work for other people have come to expect employment as a right and not a contract. They expect the benefits that the laws have mandated as their due, whether the company is profitable or not. This cannot continue and it won't because there is a relatively new concept on the horizon. It is the "business of one" where each of us is his own company and each of us is his own businessperson. It will become the new relationship once it is understood how it can be accomplished without getting oneself into trouble with the government.

The history of employment can be traced over its development of thousands of years. It runs from Master/Slave to Master/Servant (the indentured slave) to Employer/Employee. Employer/Employee is a master servant concept where the employee is an indentured slave (<u>controlled</u> by the employer as a matter of definition) but only for 8 (or however many) hours a day that the employee is under the employer's thumb.

The new kid on the block—but not really because the concept dates back to the Guilds of England where the tradesmen were uncontrolled in the manner of their work—is the independent contractor. Traditionally, the professions have also acted in an independent manner. The concept of a business of one is the self-employed relationship or the Service Recipient/Service Provider relationship.

By its very definition it is not a relationship controlled by the hiring agent, who may only have control over the end product produced by the independent contractor. Independent contractors and those who hire them are not subject to the laws imposed on the employment relationship. The law of contract is the only law that applies because the relationship is contractual and not legally imposed, as is the case with employment.

In the late 1960's and early 1970's, the Federal Government attempted to destroy the concept of independent contractors by forcing those who hired them to withhold the taxes required of employers—the so-called dreaded Taxation at its Source. Taxation at its Source (withholding) makes employers the collection agents of the government.

Witholding—the idea of a fellow with the unlikely name of Beardsley Rummel—was supposed to be only an emergency short term World War II measure. Milton Friedman, economist and Nobel Laureate, who was partially responsible for its enactment, has stated that it was the worst mistake of his lengthy career and he is ashamed of his involvement in its enactment.

In the 1970's the IRS started a special project aimed at turning everybody into an employee for withholding tax purposes. Massive assessments were levied against companies who were only left off the hook if they agreed to contribute to the Nixon re-election committee and treat their workers in the future as employees.

Well the Federal Government's attempt to destroy independent contractors failed. It is a long story why this occurred but suffice it to state that the government is no longer interested in the fight. The matter has evolved so that the government (the politicians not the bureaucrats) recognizes that independent contractors are a fact of business and it can't be stopped. Everybody is outsourcing to independent contractors. If the practice were ended some of the world's largest companies would go broke.

Not all workers will qualify for independent contractor status but it is a positive work arrangement in most cases. For the Service Recipient the independent contractor operation means that it will build alliances and build their businesses not their overhead. The following advantages for the SR are sure to be part of the transformation:

1. Flexibility
2. Specific expertise
3. Cost cutting-monetary advantages
4. Tax benefits
5. Inapplicable regulations
6. Unfounded lawsuits and adversarial relationships
7. Forced continued employment of unsuitable workers
8. Elimination of expensive benefits
9. Elimination of costly accounting services and governmentally mandated record keeping
10. Discontinuation of demeaning personnel practices such as drug testing
11. Workers who lack necessary skill
12. Elimination of negligence liability under most circumstances

For the SP the following are the advantages:
1. Flexibility/control of benefits
2. Greater pay
3. Job security
4. Be own boss
5. More concern for family obligations
6. Tax benefits—Schedule C
7. Own decisions regarding insurance and pensions

The government recognizes that its welfare programs, as we know them, will end if everybody becomes wealthy and being your own business is a way to become wealthy. Furthermore, the reason often cited for the battle to eliminate independent contractors no longer exists. Independent contractors pay their taxes and the IRS now cross-matches 1099 forms.

Moreover, the government is having problems with the payroll system in that many companies are starting up, collecting but not paying their withholding taxes. They take the money from their employees, fold up, disappear and never pay over the money. It has been estimated in the Senate Hearing on the subject that over $50 billion has been lost to the government this way and the figure is rising. Since the employer has taken the money from the employees, the government still has to credit the employee with the withheld money. Therefore, it is a double loss to the government because they have to payout the social security and unemployment money they never receive.

But why is this subject still mostly a secret? Well, there is an inbuilt reaction to change. There are those who will counsel not to change because their self-interest is at stake. It has been estimated that a changeover of a business to an independent contractor operation will save 20%o on accounting overhead. The only paperwork required of the Service Recipient is the 1099 form at the end of the year (and this is not required for payments to corporations) providing the total amount paid.

Obviously the accountants who make their money filling out the endless paper forms required for the payroll system will not benefit from any change. Banks will no longer receive their automatic payroll deposits. Moreover, the lawyers, who are naturally resistant to change, will tell their clients that to change will reap them the government's winds of wrath.

The truth is that new rules have resulted in the federal government not involving itself in payroll enforcement activity related to the I.C. issue since 1996. The problem will not be with the Feds if it is properly done. And it must be emphasized that there are rules that have to be strictly followed. Problems may exist with the State regulations, which vary from state to state. However, if one is an independent contractor for federal law purposes, it is more than likely to be so for state law purposes.

CHAPTER 4

THE BIRTH OF THE SAFE HARBOR TEST—A VICTORY FOR THE AMERICAN PEOPLE

This is an edited version of Chapter 11 of my Book, "In the Teeth of the Wind—A Study of Power and How to Fight It." The Book is available at my website **http://thelawyer.info** in case you haven't already received the message.

The businessman was my mentor on economic and behavioral, matters, although he was only a few years older than me. He is a very wise man and he shared his wisdom with me. For that and his friendship through some very rough years, I will be forever grateful. Most of all, we beat the bastards—all of them.

I call him the businessman because that's what he likes to be called. His acumen as a businessman is great, although the monetary rewards have not been as good as the acumen. If you want to increase your sales, he is available for consulting. See his website at **www.salesgeneration.com**. Because the socialistic age does not like business, being a businessman has taken on negative connotations.

He was in the telephone solicitation business. His company, Tabcor Sales Clearing, Inc., sold tickets to various kinds of shows, like clowns, magic, etc. He put these shows on for various organizations, such as Am Vets. He, also, put on a sporting event, called wheelchair sports—paraplegics who played basketball from their wheelchairs.

He wasn't enemy number one, but someone wanted to put him out of business. Simultaneously, the IRS and the Illinois Attorney General's Office sued him, separately. The businessman determined he had to fight to survive and he had to fight with whatever weapon he could devise. I was that weapon.

I am not so certain that he couldn't have gone out of business and started again in something else. But there was a certain sense of honor in him and a belief that you had to fight back when you are attacked.

Most small businessmen would have folded early. They don't know how to fight a legal war. Moreover, they don't pick lawyers like me. Since most businessmen don't know how to fight, they either cave in or they fight a losing fight and they ruin their businesses while they are fighting.

This guy knew how to fight. He put his business on a war footing. I was his chief of staff and field commander. He had to make enough money to keep his staff happy and, also, to pay me. All the while he had to make himself and his time available to me for my calls at anytime when I needed information on his business, which when examined closely is highly complex. Time and money have to be budgeted very carefully and the business must survive and improve to have any hope of surviving a litigation sledgehammer.

The key, he felt, to making his business more competitive was his use of delivery and sales staff as independent contractors and not as employees. The reasons for this are clear: greater gross pay to the workers, no IRS payroll expense, no perks, greater quality control of the product, etc.

On the other hand, the IRS wants everybody to be on the payroll system for obvious reasons: control, control, and control. Other reasons include: information (statistics), knowledge, ease of tax collection, cash flow to the banking system and power.

If totally implemented their system would wreck the American economic system. We will become slaves to their system. All the money for all of the government programs will eventually be collected as payroll. It is too easy for them to resist. But the employment system is now outdated and they can't stop the move to Independent Contractors.

You would be surprised how much our free enterprise system depends on independent contractors and it is increasing. General Motors and other large companies could not survive without them.

In 1970 and later years the IRS started a campaign to turn all independent contractors into employees. They started their attack slowly going after little fish like the businessman in order to establish precedent before they moved on to the large companies, who could afford a defense. However, eventually they hit the real large companies and it was stopped. They had gone too far, as is always the case, and our litigation with them proved embarrassing because we called it an attack on America.

Since part of his business was considered to be a charitable solicitation. The law considered him to be a "professional" fund-raiser, and he was an entity regulated by the State Attorney General's Office. The real purpose of the law is to create, by selective enforcement, a monopoly of authorized charities—the big ones like United Way. Charities are a closed racket.

The law really treats professional fund-raisers like criminals. However, by calling them "professional", the law appears to be conferring a benefit on them. White is black and black is white.

The businessman was required to register, file his contracts with his clients and, also, to provide detailed financial information. When enough information is accumulated—the bureaucracy can take all the time they want (after all, they are paid a salary to do this stuff and they call themselves public "servants")—the strike comes with front page newspaper chronicles about "charity cheats."

Although I didn't find out about it until much later, The Charitable Trusts and Solicitations Division of Illinois (as well as all the other States) was linked to the Charitable Organizations Division of the IRS. No wonder they both attacked at the same time.

The IRS through its tax regulation of charities who register as Section 501 (c) organizations link with the State Charity Offices. The IRS thereby directly controls the use to which tax-free moneys of religions and not for profit organizations can be put. It was recently ruled that witches in Salem are a tax free religious organization to show how ridiculous this has become. Moreover, it is a euphemism to call an organization not for profit because they too like all organizations must make a profit. In their case, the profits are used to pay salaries and fringe benefits and a lot of other stuff.

It appeared that the IRS wanted to bolster the social security rolls, wanted to assure the banks a source of deposits (which the withholding laws require), and wanted businesses to collect the taxes for the IRS (that being easier than individual collections). Let me state for clarification purposes, because this is really complicated stuff, that a business is not required to collect taxes on independent contractors just because they are that, namely independent and not slaves like employees.

The difference between an independent contractor and an employee is similar to the difference between a free man and a slave under the Master/Servant law. An employee is nothing more than a glorified slave, according to the law.

There was more to this IRS plan that fell into the political realm. It was something that Nixon and his cohorts got into, as a side gig to raise money—something at which they were without equal. One of Nixon's tapes record that he stated, "Wait till we sic the IRS on them."

This meant that the IRS would issue a massive assessment for claimed back withholding taxes; a settlement would ensue and the company would pay a fraction of the assessment along with an agreement to pay withholding taxes on its employees in the future. Of course, a large campaign contribution accompanied the settlement.

Special IRS employment tax schools were created and special tax projects were instituted. Some 30 industries that had historically treated its workers as independent contractors, such as, insurance agents, nurses, direct sales (door to door), real estate agents, etc., were bombed by the IRS. The excuse used was that the IRS couldn't collect what was due to them from the independent contractors; that is, since they are independent, they are bad taxpayers. Most of the businesses caved in. They couldn't afford to fight or so they thought.

But we didn't cave in; we attacked. We weren't the only ones who fought but we were the roughest and dirtiest. We called it the way it was. Eventually, the highest levels of Congress got involved. The politicians were told to end it lest it severely impact on the American Economy. They were forced to end the bureaucratic power moves, because General Motors and other such companies were forcing them on one end and we were hitting them low on the other.

At first, powerful leaders of the Senate (on both sides of the aisle, namely, Bob Dole of Kansas and Russell Long) started making floor speeches. The usually arrogant IRS ignored the warning and forced Congress to enact Section 530 of the Revenue Act of 1978—a very unusual law—not publicized by the press for what it really was—a legislative moratorium ("Don't do it") on an administrative agency.

We always felt that our efforts were in large part the cause of a lot of this legislative movement. We had been called to "testify" in Washington, D.C. about this before the very powerful and enigmatic Joint committee on Taxation. They thought we were crazy when we asked for "reparations" and the "termination" of the agent involved. It was an utter victory for the forces of light.

We were also called before a special Senate Committee investigating IRS abuses. Senator Carlos Montoya of New Mexico headed a task force on the subject. Little of what came out was ever publicized. Senator

Montoya himself was attacked by the IRS and, apparently died a broken though honest man. The IRS did the same thing to Idaho Congressman George Hansen. Here are some highlights of that testimony:
(After testifying that the IRS agent had served an IRS subpoena at the home of the businessman)
"Senator Montoya. Do you consider that a harassment?
Businessman. More than harassment, Senator.
Senator Montoya. And who was the target of the administrative summons, you or your wife?
Businessman. Both me and my wife on our personal return, because we file jointly. And (my company) was the only target, as he again said later in court, he was not interested in our personal return only (my company).
Senator Montoya. Was she an officer of (your company)?
Businessman. Not in any way. My wife was pregnant. She proceeded to bleed internally for a week after that and spent several days in the hospital and had to be operated on and it turned into a miscarriage.
Senator Montoya. Was that as a result of this?
Businessman. It was directly following it. She was served these summonses incidentally. forcibly through the door into her stomach. This was the back door; made a run, like a run in through the door, shoved it in her stomach. She had no idea what they were. He just said "Sally", and it sounded like someone who was familiar, and shoved it in her stomach. He turned around and walked back toward the car that had another man in it, apparently an agent, and they both stood by the car laughing at my wife and then they left."

As I said, my client had been hit twice at the same time. The State case was the first of the two with which I became involved. I later got involved with the Federal tax case that was also ongoing at the time. The State case threatened to close my client's operation down because they were seeking an injunction to stop him from conducting any business.

The businessman's state case took only six years. The federal tax case went on for thirteen years before it too whimpered away. The federal case was not one case; it was really seven separate cases. Over the years, the government involved well over one hundred lawyers to handle the various cases.

This too is a trick of theirs. It keeps each lawyer from becoming too friendly and, also, each time a new lawyer took over, he would say that he needed more time to acquaint himself with the case. They come up with one joke after another.

The battle was over whether my client could treat workers as independent contractors (I.C.'s) or whether he had to declare them to be employees. If they were employees the business was liable for employment taxes (which include: income tax, FICA (social security), and FUTA (federal unemployment) taxes. If they were independent contractors, they themselves were liable for everything except FUTA taxes, which were only paid if the individual was an employee.

The test of whether somebody is an employee or an independent contractor is an enormously complicated factual matter. It involves the examination of 20 different factors, called the 20 common law factor test.

Our efforts were never publicized. Nor was there a big victory and my grinning face was never seen on TV. news. Most cases end in whimpers or in the most bizarre twists one can imagine. In my case, the IRS and its DOJ's (Department of Justice's) counterpart the dreaded Tax Division (the blue bloods with pin-stripe suits) did their damnedest to prevent a trial and they were successful.

A trial would have shown that there was a plot to destroy the independent American businessman. The case caused Congress to become involved. How this came about is now a part of American History—like others—that has been kept hidden from the public.

As in so many of these types of cases, what was really happening was shielded from public scrutiny by the use of doublespeak and gobbledy gook so that the Congressional moratorium preventing the IRS from continuing with their plot appeared to be only a technical matter buried within the mammoth so-called Tax Reform Act of 1978. In fact, the moratorium represented a great victory for the American people over the tax bureaucrats.

The politicians, who rely on the bureaucrats for their power, were forced to take sides against them. This was a rare occurrence. It does show where the real power is, however. If the politicians wanted to exercise real control, an organized citizenry can force them to act.

Because of Section 530, the court was forced to decide the case in our favor. We received the first judgment ever that my client's business was protected by Section 530 (the Safe Harbor). It was a complete victory without a trial. However, it was not the end of the case.

We decided to try to get back all the fees I was paid. This started a whole new war. At the time, because of Watergate, laws had been passed which allowed persons who had been wrongly attacked by government to recoup their costs. The purpose was, allegedly, to equalize the power of and to deter wrongful conduct by the bureaucracy. Unfortunately, as expected, it has not been fairly applied and all kinds of restrictions have been placed on it.

It is interesting for me to look back and realize that in none of the political science courses that I took in college was there ever a serious discussion about the bureaucracy. And yet, they are the army of government. The Courts are a bureaucracy. Naturally, they would side step any attempt to equalize the battle between the people and the bureaucracy.

Although we had won our case in 1978, the fee battle continued for a longtime. We lost after a three day trial in which the judge found that the IRS had not acted in "bad faith." We had proven that the agent had committed perjury but that was not enough.

After the trial but before the judge's decision, pressure had been put on him by the Justice Department. He was on our side but apparently he had his skeletons. An uncomplimentary article about him appeared in a buried newspaper article—something about a Federal investigation into his conduct about something or other. He apologized to me for ruling against us but he explained the pressure that was put on him. In other words, the fee case was fixed against us. I can prove it.

We had also filed a damage case against the IRS agent, who had physically caused the businessman's wife to have a miscarriage. The lawsuit was broader than that and included an allegation that the IRS had intentionally attempted to destroy the businessman's business.

I caused a subpoena to be served on Laurence Woodworth, then Assistant Secretary of the Treasury for Tax Policy. Attached to the subpoena was a list of questions that related to the illegal IRS re-classification program. A Deputy U.S. Marshall served the subpoena in Washington, D.C. I heard from the Deputy that immediately after service of these papers, Mr. Woodworth dropped dead of a stroke. I guess we got a little too close to the truth—death by subpoena.

The lawsuit, however, was dismissed based on an affidavit filed by the agent, a proven perjurer, that he had acted in good faith. A mockery was again made of the Seventh Amendment right to a jury trial. Judges are naturally deferential to the IRS.

Although the federal courts profess that government agents are to be treated the same as private citizens that is not the case. The reason for this is, at least partly, because the courts are not truly a separate branch of government. It was intended that they be so by our founders; however, they are not financially self-sustaining, but are subsidized by Congress.

This makes them beholden to the "system" and they preserve and protect it. The only way to change this club system is to make the courts self-sufficient and financially independent and remove the Federal Judge's lifetime appointment. Gerry Spence's idea of rotating judges selected from a pool of trial lawyers is a very good idea.

In all my client spent several hundred thousand dollars fighting a fight that never should have begun. Luckily, his business prospered all throughout the fight, strange as it may seem. We beat them all.

PART II

FOR INDIVIDUALS

CHAPTER 5

WHY BE AN INDEPENDENT CONTRACTOR

Being an IC is not for everybody. If you have the knowledge and desire to be your own boss—it is the only way to go. Why? Because the advantages of IC and self-employment status far outweigh those of the ES, not only in compensatory advantage but, also, the non-material freedom advantages that the IC status provides.

It is assumed that by purchasing this book, you are already interested in at least exploring this subject to determine whether it is for you and how to do it. Of course, we are dealing with a transformation and in all such paradigm shifts, change has come about slowly because resistance to it has been powerful, as is always the case. Those endowed with the *status quo* (particularly lawyers and other so-called tax professionals) resist with all of their might, rather than get on board to advance the clear IC trend in employment.

Along with the advantages of IC status, comes the task of being responsible for oneself. This is something that we, as proud Americans, have gotten away from. We have been taught that it is the responsibility of the government or our "employer" to care for us. A surge of self-reliance has come about recently because we all know there is too much Big Brother.

This is the concept of a "Business of One". Gerry Spence called it a "Union of One" but I like Business of One better. This is what the IC business is all about—you as an IC must take care of yourself. That means you must insure that you are adequately paid so that you can pay for what you need that the SR (unless provided for in the IC agreement) and the government will no longer provide, such as:

General liability ("umbrella") or Errors and Omissions insurance;
Severance pay or building a stash;
Disability insurance;
Medical and Dental;
Pensions;
Continuing education.

The advantages and benefits to which you are entitled as an IC, both pecuniary and in lifestyle are as follows:

1. You will be able to take the tax deductions from gross income not allowed to employees. See your local tax advisor or contact us.
2. You will only have to make quarterly tax payments but even those under certain circumstance do not have to be made. Ask your tax advisor or ask us about it. Even so, the penalty for not doing so is small.
3. You will build up your assets and provide yourself with the necessary specialized training to assist you in your business, the purchases of which will be tax deductible, increasing your productivity and value to your customers and establishing that you are entitled to increasing amounts of pay.

4. You will be able to add to your customer base, thereby ensuring continued work in the event of slowdowns and acquire greater job security.
5. You will be able to arrange your own insurance needs, according to your own preferences.
6. You will have the flexibility to determine when you want to take your vacations and time off work.
7. You will be your own boss.
8. You will determine your own retirement plans and will be eligible for a Keough Plan (HR10) which will enable you to deduct 25% of your gross income up to $30,000 per year to go into your retirement account. Additionally you will be in full control as to how your retirement funds are invested. You will also be eligible for various IRA plans. For further information on this subject contact your local financial advisor or contact us.

The biggest benefit that an IC enjoys is in most cases, although not a necessity as far as the rules go, is the ability to work for more than one SR, thus ensuring continuing pay in the event one SR reduces staff, the task is finished, or the SR goes out of business

The trend is away from the ES, especially during periods like we are undergoing. Along with the changing landscape of the enormous effects of the technology revolution (the information age-considered to be our third economic revolution after "farming and "industrial") has come the changing concepts of people towards their work. You will be in control of your work rather than "the company." It is in your interest to work as hard as you can.

The ES is outdated, encumbered as it has become, with all of the laws that have been piled on it. It has led to low productivity and endless work conflicts. It was meant to apply to a centralized workforce system where everybody went to work at a certain location and started and ended at a certain time with detailed instructions given as to how the work was to be done. The ES is not conducive to the decentralized work system that we are now entering.

Work has become task oriented with teams of IC specialists accomplishing a task put before them by the SR. How you, as an IC, do your work is not important, as long as the task is satisfactorily completed within parameters established for the end product within a time frame set by the SR.

The laws engrafted onto the ES, mostly of recent origin, have tolled the bell on the death of that system. However, there will be a continuing need for employees, such as secretaries, unless they have their own secretarial business and work for more than just one company in which case they would be IC/SP's on their own. Companies need certain people to be controlled as to hours and performance of jobs. The lack of the right to control an IC, as hereafter explained, is the difference in the work of an IC as against an employee. Certain people have a need to work in such a controlled environment where they are told how, when, and where to perform their work. We assume you are not one who wants to be an employee or else you would not be interested in this Book.

The laws meant to protect the employee from all manner of conceivable alleged injuries in fact produce a slave and conflict oriented mentality toward work. These laws do not apply to the IC status. However, self-protection according to what you choose and want to pay for and not what the SR is willing to provide is a goal you should achieve.

We hope you find this Book an easy way to understand what has been made to appear as a complicated subject. Simplicity is what we are striving for because so many others have attempted to make it the subject of fear as a barrier to making the transformation. Some of these alleged "how to do it" books contain hundreds of pages of complicated explanations of what is really a simple matter.

Most of you have chosen through the purchase of this Book to convert to IC status or to assure that your own conversion has been properly done. In this regard we will do our best to assist you, if you contact us with a question. However, self-help always has its own risks. In addition to the advice in the Book, Freedom Lawyers of America offers a money back guarantee and certification procedure, whereby our IC Member Specialists will certify that you are an IC, which will protect you against any problems you may have with anybody over any question of the propriety of your IC status. For more information about our services check our website at **http://thelawyer.info** or call me at 269-207-6219.

CHAPTER 6

REQUIREMENTS FOR IC STATUS

If you work for somebody who has the right to control your work, you are an employee. In the IC situation, the SR only has the right to receive a quality end product or service.

It is always difficult to explain a complicated subject simply. But that is the purpose of this Book. There are two laws that provide the mandatory requirements for IC treatment. One is called the 20CLFT and the other the SHT. The 20CLFT is the most complicated test known to the law because no one or combination of factors controls. The determination is made by looking at the IC's relationship to all of the factors as a whole.

The 20CLFT is used by the IRS to determine whether you are an IC. State laws pretty much conform to this test also in one variety or another. Specific information will be provided about your State, if you ask us. For most purposes, if you qualify for the IRS, you will qualify for your State.

In addition to the 20CLFT, Congress because it was angry at the IRS' attempt to destroy IC's in the late 1970's and early 80's, passed an interim measure know as Section 530 of the Revenue Act of 1978, the SHT. This law was reenacted each year until 1982 when in revised form it was made permanent by the Tax Equity and Fiscal Responsibility Act of 1982.

If you are a certain type of "techie" specialist who is brokered to other companies you were made a "statutory employee," as are others: government workers; food and laundry delivery drivers (unless they own their own business); certain types of at home workers who are supplied with the materials they use; full-time salespersons who sell goods for resale; and corporate officers.

However, a new IRS Chief Counsel's opinion allows corporate officers to be IC's to their corporation. Certain occupations are "statutory IC's", such as: real estate agents, if they have a written IC Agreement with their Brokers; and direct sellers of consumer products, if they have a written IC Agreement with their suppliers. This will be discussed in a later Chapter.

According to the legislative history of the 1982 Act, it is to be <u>liberally construed in favor</u> of the one claiming to be an IC. Additionally, pursuant to the Small Business Jobs Protection Act of 1996, for periods after 1996, the IRS is required to bear the burden of proof that an individual is <u>not</u> an IC.

The SHT is called that because if you come within its protective (in other words safe harbor) provisions, you are automatically an IC. That is the present and simply put status of the law. Now for the nitty gritty—the absolute bottom-line requirements.

The SHT does not replace the 20CLFT; it only supplanted it—and became an umbrella of protection for IC's. It is only important for you to remember that if you qualify under the 20CLFT, that is a "reasonable basis" under the SHT and you automatically qualify. The IRS will not be able to reclassify you. The SHT applies only to companies but they are the ones who need the protection of the SHT because the IRS never goes after the individual.

So the only question that remains is what are the absolutely necessary factors out of the 20 with which you will need to comply. In the 1996 IRS Training Manual, the IRS loosened its interpretation of the 20CLFT for fear of further Congressional restrictions. The IRS recognized for the first time that being an IC "can be a valid and appropriate business choice."

Certain of the 20 factors are no longer important to the IRS. Those used to be the difficult ones. These are the critical factors:

1. <u>You offer your services to the public</u>—advertising in a local newspaper, grocery bulletin board, flyers, yellow pages, etc. Just because you advertise does not mean you have to accept jobs from those who may call you. Besides you should want as many customers as you can handle.
2. <u>You must have a written agreement</u> with each SR indicating your intent to be an IC and that you are permitted to work for other SR's, if you so desire. The particulars of this agreement are supposed to be negotiated fairly between you and the SR and can include other benefits besides pay. I can provide representation to you to negotiate with your SR in order to assure you receive the best deal possible.
3. <u>You must own or rent your own equipment.</u>
4. <u>You must invoice your billings</u> . Your pay can be hourly, daily, weekly, monthly, yearly, flat fee, bonus, incentives, etc. Flat fee payable in increments is preferable but not a necessity. A simple invoice is all that is necessary but you must invoice your SR, preferably on a periodic basis but never the same days.
5. <u>You should have unreimbursed business expenses</u> reportable as deductions from Gross Income on IRS Schedule C.
6. Although not a requirement for you, the SP, but required of the SR, <u>the SHT requires that the SR, who retains your services, must file 1099 forms with the IRS at the end of the calendar year</u>. Penalties for failure to file 1099 forms are negligible. The SHT also provides that you can't be an employee and an IC for the same "period", meaning quarterly period.
7. Although not mandatory, <u>it would be best for you to incorporate and sign a management services agreement with your corporation</u>. I can provide this service. Payments from one corporation to another do not require the filing of 1099 forms. However, in any event you must have

a business presence whether it is sole proprietorship with registration with your county clerk under the assumed name law or a partnership or any other entity such as the new limited liability companies.

Well that is it. It is easy. However, if you desire additional protection, we can provide it for a reasonable fee. As stated FloA's IC Specialists will provide you with the Certification and Money Back Guarantee procedure previously explained. The Certification procedure by our nationwide Member Specialists takes advantage of Court interpretations that reasonable reliance on a professional's opinion constitutes a "reasonable basis," according to the SHT.

The Courts have stated:

"(The SR's) reliance on the advice of professional tax advisors (that its SP's were IC's under the 20CLFT) is sufficient to demonstrate a reasonable basis under (the SHT) for not treating its (IC's) as employees...reliance upon the professional advice rendered by the (tax professional) constitutes a reasonable basis..."

"Generally, the courts have found that reasonable cause exists where the taxpayer relied on the advice of a trusted attorney or accountant. (Citing authority). Indeed in this regard, the Supreme Court has stated that:"

'When an accountant or attorney advises a taxpayer on a matter of tax law, such as whether a liability exists, it is reasonable for the taxpayer to rely on that advice. Most taxpayers are not competent to discern error in the substantive advice of an accountant or attorney. To require the taxpayer to challenge the attorney, to seek a "second opinion," or try to monitor counsel on the provisions of the Code himself would nullify the very purpose of seeking advice of a presumed expert in the first place. "Ordinary business care and prudence" do not demand such actions."(Citing Supreme Court case)."

We provide IC specialty tax professional advice for a fee in the form of a personal visit to your location, money back guarantee, and a certification that will provide you with the necessary reliance on our advice, which constitutes the SHT's reasonable basis. Our analysis will provide the advice that you qualify for IC status under the 20CLFT.

If you are already an employee with your company but want your company to convert to an IC system, we can provide that assistance. Show this Book to your boss as a starter. Better yet, buy another one.

PART III

FOR COMPANIES

CHAPTER 7

WHY IT IS A NECESSITY FOR YOUR BUSINESS TO USE INDEPENDENT CONTRACTORS

The following advantages for the SR are sure to continue to impel the IC Revolution:
1. Flexibility
2. Specific expertise
3. Cost cutting-monetary advantages
4. Tax benefits
5. Many laws and regulations do not apply to IC's.
    a. Pensions-ERISA—Employee Retirement Income Security Act. *Community for Creative Non-Violence v. Reed*, 490 U.S. 730 (1989).
    b. ADA-Americans with Disability Act.

c. NLRA—National Labor Relations Act—*NLRB v. United Insurance Co.*, 390 U.S. 254 (1968).
   d. FLSA—Fair Labor Standards Act—*Tony and Susan Alamo Foundation v. Secy. Of Labor*, 471 U.S. 290 (1985).
   e. INS (Immigration and Naturalization Service) regulations.
   f. EEOC—Equal Employment Opportunity Commission—Title VII of the Civil Rights Act of 1964. *Kirby v. Swimfashions*, 904 F.2d 36 (6th Cir. 1990).
   g. State Workers Compensation Acts.
   h. ADEA—Age Discrimination in Employment. Act. *Lorilard v. Pons*, 434 U.S. 575 (1978).
   i. OSHA—Occupation Safety and Health Act—*Cochran v. International Harvester Co.*, 408 F. Supp.598 (W.D., Ky, 1975).
   j. Family Leave Act.
   k. Mandated vacation days.
6. An end to frivolous lawsuits and adversarial relationships
7. An end to forced continued employment of unsuitable workers
8. Elimination of expensive benefits
9. Elimination of costly accounting services and governmentally mandated record keeping
10. Discontinuation of demeaning personnel practices such as drug testing
11. No need to keep workers who lack necessary skills
12. Elimination of negligence liability under most circumstances
13. IC's do not belong to unions

If that doesn't convince company honchos to get on board, I don't know what will do it. Especially with the insurance FloA offers, I think companies who don't take the leap could be criticized by their shareholders for not doing so.

CHAPTER 8

RESISTANCE TO CHANGE CAUSES TRADITIONAL ADVISORS NEGATIVITY

As stated by Sam Walton, the founder of Wal-Mart in his autobiography, "Made in America", who made constant change the number one priority of his business:

"I've made it my own personal mission to ensure that constant change is a vital part of the Wal-Mart culture itself. I've forced change—sometimes for change's sake alone—at every turn in our company's development. In fact, I think one of the greatest strengths of Wal-Mart's ingrained culture is its ability to drop everything and turn on a dime."

Accountants want to continue with payroll; they are not as concerned as are you in devising ways to save you money. They are concerned with making money themselves and payroll is very lucrative for them.

Lawyers are known as the most regressive of the professions in terms of accommodating to change for a number of reasons, most of which relates to the concept that, "We have always done it this way, so why change."

These advisors will think of a million reasons why you should not change. Don't listen to them, unless they give you good reasons. Then let us know what they tell you and we will provide you with the legal support you need to counter their arguments. IC status is legal and easy to accomplish and risk free, if done properly.

Lawyers and accountants often cite to the example of Microsoft's famous case as a reason not to convert. However, a reading of the case produces a different result. Realizing the cost effectiveness of ICs, Microsoft attempted to convert some of its employees to ICs. Their lawyers knew that it was improper because the workers did not qualify as ICs. The IRS questioned the conversions and Microsoft admitted that they were really employees. The IRS reclassified them.

Upon hearing of Microsoft's IRS admission, the reclassified employees got together and sued Microsoft, claiming that they were entitled to the employee benefits that other Microsoft employees received. Microsoft had to pay them a large amount of money. The moral is not that IC conversions are improper; rather, the moral is that it has to be properly done and for the right reasons. Microsoft's lawyers did them a great deal of damage because they didn't provide their client with the correct advice. The Microsoft case is not a reason for you to fear an IC conversion.

Allstate was recently sued by a group of salesmen who claim they were "coerced" into becoming ICs. Allstate denies the claim and it is probable that this case will be in the Courts for years to come. Well, it should be obvious that coercion should not be involved. If the worker does not want to be an IC and obtain the many benefits therefrom, he is obviously not a good candidate for IC treatment.

CHAPTER 9

A BUSINESSMAN'S PERSPECTIVE

The fact that you are considering using IC's in your business should be only one aspect of an overall plan to make your business an efficient and profitable operation. It is not enough that your business is doing well if none of the profit is going into your pockets. Unfortunately, so many business advisors and accountants do not understand this.

It is often difficult for a business owner to see the inefficiencies in his own business and, therefore, outside consulting is necessary. It is not the purpose of this article, nor is it possible, to analyze all of the requirements for an efficient and profitable business because each business is unique. If you want a glimpse into the near future get the recent works of management and business guru, Peter Drucker.

However, we believe that the use of IC's is the first step to the organization of a sound business operation. It is not only a reduction of cost item; it is a structural change, which will make your business more efficient and will make your SPs happier and more independent. Why this is the case will now be discussed.

As I am sure you are all aware, the term outsourcing is relatively new. Yet, it signifies what is happening. Companies are outsourcing all extraneous practices so that they can stress their core competencies. The movement toward the use of IC's is just a small part of the outsourcing movement. Employee leasing and contingent workforces, however, are more expensive and have many more drawbacks than the use of ICs.

Our employment structure is undergoing massive change. The new technologies are changing it. We are quickly becoming one world. Geographic boundaries are and will be quickly evaporating. Information control is no longer possible. The old power bases are dissolving. Income and sales taxes are no longer viable. Social Security is a highly visible and unresolved problem.

There is no such thing any longer as a lifetime job. Changes are averaging every five years. Pensions, health and life insurance in order to be worthwhile need to be owned by the individual worker. Companies can and do go bankrupt. This is the concept of the free market that allows new businesses to thrive.

Information and knowledge belong to the individual, not to the company. Knowledge can be copied and it is mobile. The new knowledge worker—the Business of One—has provided us with the greatest increase in productivity in the history of the world. Businesses that operate the old way are doomed to failure.

The outstanding feature of America's continuing economic miracle is freedom of choice, despite the tendency of government to limit freedom. We always seem to find a way around the restrictions thrown at us by the politicians and bureaucrats.

The key to building a successful business in this new age is to build alliances not adversaries and the people who work for you are your allies and they need to be kept happy. Build your business not your overhead. Make yourself into a virtual business. The advantages to an IC operation have already been explained to you. Take the plunge and free yourself.

Accountants and lawyers are basically nitpickers. They are good at undoing things but poor at devising new ways of doing things. Why is it that lawyers, doctors, court reporters, most accountants, etc. are considered ICs? Do they know something that we don't?

The following details some of the factors that are necessary for you to analyze. We would like you to use the businessman's consulting services (See, www.salesgeneration.com for marketing and other business advice) to help bring about any changes you might need.

The following needs to be analyzed according to four factors—time, cost, people and space.

1. State the objectives—what products to what markets at what rates.
2. Take inventory of present status.
3. Make estimates for each objective—timing and costs.
4. Set up operation (or reorganize) for each objective.
5. Market contact lists and databases.
6. Hire IC's and management—using profiles and filters.
7. Train people—training programs and Books.
8. Presentations (the message) and sales Books.
9. Install Sales Maintenance and Results Systems.
10. Schedules and Projects.
11. Sales materials flow.
13. Order processing, pay processing.
14. Results and history data and links.
15. Install feedback, control and expert systems.
    Internal to/for
        Management.
        Sales force.
        Product lines.
        Market and market segments.
        Financial flow.

External to:
> Customers
> Outside marketing services.
> Outside accounting services.

Please feel free to call on us to help you with your business plans. We believe that the transformation to an IC operation will be a first step in putting your business into the modern era.

CHAPTER 10

CONVERSIONS

In order to convert present employees to ICs a special provision of the SHT requires that the employee's new position with your company not be substantially the same that he held as an employee. The SHT cannot be invoked for protection if your converted employee was in a "substantially similar position" before he was converted to an IC. This does not mean that he does not qualify under the 20CLFT because the 20 CLFT is separate from the SHT. But it does mean that you will have to prove the IC status under that test. We have already shown you how to do this.

But it always better to have the protection of the SHT. Therefore, what do you have to do to qualify your converted employees? Well, what does "substantially similar position" really mean? We believe it means that you must do more than just calling a person an IC, as did Microsoft.

It means a restructuring of the work that the employee did. Is he now a supervisor, a consultant, a manager, a specialist, etc? As we have stated, the use of IC's is more than a cost saving to you. It is a different way of looking at work. Give the worker a task and let him do it his way. As long as the end product is satisfactory why would you want to control him? He can rent the necessary tools from you or purchase them from you and do the job on his own.

The job that the employee now does for you has to be of a type that lends itself to the work of an IC. This requires a Change of thinking. Why do you care when your IC comes to work? If you do, then forget about IC treatment. Why do care where he does the work? If you do, then keep him as an employee. Although if it is necessary for the work to be done on site, that is okay now under the new IRS rules. Why do you care if he only works for you? If you do then keep him as an employee, although the IRS is no longer interested in multiple sources of work.

You should be interested in allowing your SP to make as much money as he desires and if you don't have enough work for him, let him get other work. If there are secrets you don't want him to share with other companies, that can be take care of with a proper secrecy clause in the IC Agreement.

If the employee doesn't understand the advantages you are providing to him by allowing him to work as an IC, then don't try to convert him to an IC. He won't hack it. And coercion can't be involved, unless you want to buy a lawsuit, as did Allstate. As part of our services, FLoA will confer with your prospective IC to provide him with a benefits package that will explain why IC status is good for him, as well as for your company. We can also assist you in the restructuring of your work.

CHAPTER 11

ACCOUNTING AND TAX SAVING TIPS FOR THE SERVICE PROVIDER AND SERVICE RECIPIENT

The independent contractor operation is a model of accounting efficiency and tax savings. The SR is probably more attuned to accounting needs than is the SP because as a business owner, you have been required to keep books. The SP may or may not be unfamiliar with accounting practices and the tax accounting aspect of running his business. These are some of the tips for you.

You are no longer bound to do payroll, except for those left as employees, and it may be wise to maintain a few. It is suggested that some of the staff should still be considered employees and payroll done for them but it is not absolutely necessary, except for payments you may receive as a corporate officer, if you own a corporation. It is no longer necessary to make withholding bank deposits for the IC's—payments should be in accordance with invoices received on an intermittent basis (not absolutely necessary but recommended).

Only form necessary for IC's is the 1096 and 1099s for each of the IC's.

An accountant is not necessary to complete these simple forms. Quickbooks software is recommended for businesses.

No matching Social Security Medicare for IC's. Cost saving of .0765 % of payroll.

Unemployment (FUTA) costs are eliminated—varies between 2.7%-10% of payroll.

Fringe benefits can be eliminated to the extent desired or kept as the case may be.

The intangible cost saving of all the paperwork and legal restrictions attached to the employer/employee relationship and the tangible cost of workman's compensation insurance savings.

The following are some of the tips that you can advise your SPs that will be available to them. If the SP understands the benefits of an IC relationship, he is not apt to claim "coercion" or to file lawsuits. The relationship is subject to arms length bargaining.

1. Schedule C entitlement for deductions of business related expenses from gross income = a substantial reduction in taxable income because these expenses can only be taken on a greatly limited basis as employees. See IRS form Schedule C. Even though social security and Medicare are taxable at the full rate (15%), Form 1040, page 1 allows a deduction for one half; therefore the Social Security burden is no more than it would be for an employee paying half and employer paying half. Furthermore, Social Security tax is taken only on the net income after deduction of expenses.

Home Office expense is deductible as a percentage of total house use or as reasonable lease from owner to IC. Home office equipment, utilities and furniture are deductible either by depreciation or lease.

Car and Truck expenses are deductible based on actual cost at a percentage of usage or mileage can be used, if documented, at presently $.365 per mile. Deduction begins from their home office.

Business equipment is fully deductible (through depreciation schedules or as a lease) against gross income. Your SPs should have a computer and one of the popular accounting software programs, such as Quicken or MSMoney.

Pension plans—

2. HR 10 (Keough Plan)—<u>Only available</u> to IC's, as self-employed individuals, up to 25% of gross income for a maximum of $30,000.00. This plan is available even though the SP or his spouse are participants in another employee plan.

S.E.P. (Simplified Employee Plan)—an IC is considered an employer and employee contributions can be up to 15% of net income.

I.R.A. (Individual retirement plan)—maximum $2,000 deduction (subject to gross income limitations).

Simple Plan—subject to IRA limitations.

3. If the SP is a corporation and he is a corporate officer, he can take income both as an employee and as self-employed and wear two hats and, therefore, obtain the tax and pension advantages of both an IC and as an employee. See explanation in a later Chapter for an explanation of this or give us a call.

4. Insurance

There are again two perspectives on this subject. One is from the view of the SP and the other from the SR. The SP will in all likelihood need a greater input on this subject because he may be unfamiliar with it. Of course a lot depends on what coverages the SR has in place and what he intends on keeping.

Legally, there is an elimination of workman's compensation (which should be covered by the SP with disability insurance). Also, there is no unemployment compensation. This can be covered by an adequate severance provision in the IC agreement and adequate savings.

The SR may continue health and dental insurance or another group plan arranged.

General liability ("umbrella") or Errors and Omissions insurance;

5. Investment

Pension and investment advice is needed for both the Recipient and the Provider, especially where the Recipient is a corporation and the officers opt to be IC's to the corporation and, therefore, eligible for the great benefits of the Keogh and other plans.

The following is a brief outline of things that should be considered by your SPs. Investment counselors can provide you with additional information and FloA can provide additional advice and products.

<u>Pre-tax investing</u>.
Your tax bracket.
Power of tax deferred investing.
Principals of Compounding Interest.—Rule of 62.
The sooner the better.
Starting early.
Age against time.
Different plans
<u>Insuring for Health</u>.
Major medical and dental.
Cancer, long term care and specialized coverages
<u>Life Insurance</u>—what type and how much.
<u>Disability</u>—Long and short term.

CHAPTER 12

REQUIREMENTS FOR INDEPENDENT CONTRACTOR TREATMENT

The simplified requirements stated in Chapter 6, *supra* always remain the same.

PART IV

FOR CORPORATE OFFICERS

CHAPTER 13

DUAL HAT STATUS

It is hoped that this Chapter will provide you with information necessary to attain the dual hat Employee/Independent Contractor status that you are seeking. We assume you are already incorporated and are an officer of that corporation (President, CEO, Vice-President, Treasurer, Secretary etc.) because dual hat status only applies if you hold that status, although an SP can be an employee and an IC under the same rule.

If you are not already incorporated, it is easy to do by yourself. If there are any questions, please feel free to contact us.

The IRS has ruled that Corporate Officers, previously thought of as being exclusively statutory employees and, therefore subject to employment status, and all of its concomitant laws, rules and regulations can wear a "dual hat" and be both an employee and an IC. Your corporation is your SR and you are the SP/Employee.

What is required? You have to meet the easy but specific requirements of what constitutes an independent contractor, which has to be separate from your role as a corporate officer employee. By reading the material in this Book, you should already have an understanding of what is involved.

FLoA will help you if you have any questions about the material. If you follow a few easy steps this can be easily accomplished and we will guarantee the proper outcome, if you retain us for our Certification Procedure. But again it can be put as simply as this: "to be an IC you have to look like and be an IC."

What difference does dual status make? As an employee, you can participate in your corporation's qualified retirement plan and be eligible for fringe benefits. Getting those can be a plus. As an IC you can set up a Keogh plan and tax shelter additional amounts for ultimate retirement. You can also deduct business expenses that would, if related to employment as an employee, be deductible, if at all, as miscellaneous itemized deductions. Such deductions are subject to a 2% floor and a 3% phase out.

An additional plus that is affecting more and more taxpayers is that miscellaneous itemized deductions are not deductible at all for purposes of the Alternative Minimum Tax. Although these benefits may seem complicated, they aren't. And in the dual hat status will save you a pile of money that would otherwise go to Uncle Sam. Besides the retirement and tax benefits, already mentioned, there are others. For instance, as an IC you could attempt to get others to pay you for the services you provide to your corporation.

The task of dual hat status is to avoid interrelatedness. Your function toward your corporation must be different than the function you perform as a corporate officer. They must not be related. If you receive pay as the corporate officer, this must be reported as withholding wages. But the IC pay will be as a self-employed individual.

Most of you have chosen through the purchase of this Book to convert to dual hat status or to assure that your own conversion has been done properly. However, self-help always has its own risks. As we have repeatedly stated, perhaps too often, Freedom Lawyers of America offers a money back guarantee and certification procedure, whereby our IC Member Specialists will certify that you are an IC, which will protect you against any problems you may have with anybody over any question of the propriety of your IC status. For more information about our services check our website at www.thelawyer.info E-mail at shelly@thelawyer.info shelly@cybersol.com or call 269-207-6219.

In its IRS legal memorandum (ILM) 200038045), prepared by the IRS's Chief Counsel's Office on August 9, 2000, the IRS opined that, although a corporate officer was a "statutory employee" there was no exclusion in the SHT that prevented a corporate officer from also being an IC (SP) to his corporation (SR). Such an individual could wear "two hats." This IRS Chief Counsel's opinion, which is almost like law, provides corporate officers with a tremendous advantage over exclusive employee status.

This was a great, although almost unnoticed benefit to owners/officers of corporations. As stated by the author of the ILM, "…submission of a Form 1099 may be sufficient to establish a corporation's treatment of the officer as an independent contractor.

As we have stated lack of interrelatedness is the essence of dual hat status. There are many ways of doing this. You can be an officer of your corporation, who does the bookkeeping but, also, be a manager of your sales force or a salesman, or a board member, or a carpenter, etc—the list is without limit. The employee income part of the dual hat will be reported on Form W2 and the IC part on Form 1099.

CHAPTER 14

PROTOCOLS FOR SETTING UP YOUR OWN BUSINESS UNDER THE "TWO HAT SYSTEM"

Set up a corporation.

<u>First Hat</u>—Pay yourself a reasonable salary as a corporate officer.

<u>Second Hat</u>—Set up an IC Agreement with your corporation, which will pay you from the net profits for services rendered. Payments to be reported by the corporation to the IRS with form 1099. Payments to you are reflected on 1040 Schedule C.

25% of the gross Schedule C income but not more than $30,000 can be sheltered in a Keough pension plan, which you control.

Additionally, take this as an EXAMPLE of what can be done:

You have been in a service business for a number of years. Your wife formed a Corporation to perform her own service business.

You sell services to her corporation, pursuant to an IC Agreement. You already have health insurance. However, pursuant to the IC Agreement, your wife's corporation can pay for that. You have a cost efficient automobile, and can pay for the expenses using the standard mileage option as a Schedule C deduction. This will be beneficial both to the corporation (SR) and to me the IC (SP).

This arrangement will allow you to expense a portion of household expenses for use as a "second office" at my home.

You also have the option of starting your own retirement plan (known as a Keough or HR10). This <u>fantastic</u> plan is under your control, unlike 401k's.

And the deductible tax-free amount you can contribute to it greatly reduces taxable income by up to 25% of gross Schedule C income up to $30,000.

Also, you are shielded from an IRS audit that might deem your pay excessive, if you were paid as a corporate officer, and charge it as "disguised dividends," which are not deductible by the corporation. These disguised dividend adjustments do not apply to IC's.

You can also rent your equipment and car from the corporation

The benefits to your wife's corporation (SR) are as follows:
1. None of the complexities and expenses of payroll reporting.
2. No payroll taxes and no accounting fees to keep track of it. Just a simple 1099 at the end of the year.
3. Simple reimbursement for medical expenses;
4. Corporation doesn't have to provide you with a car.
5. You can dispense your services pursuant to the IC Agreement.
6. Corporation doesn't have to pay for Worker's Compensation Insurance.
7. Corporation won't be burdened with having to comply with all the federal and state laws applicable to employees, a costly burden in terms of time necessary to complete all the forms.

8. Corporation doesn't have to be concerned about being sued for any of the number of lawsuits permitted by employees that have so burdened the employment system (ES).

In exchange for the above listed corporate advantages, you as the self-employed SP can negotiate a higher percentage of billable fees and work for other clients, plus obtaining the tax advantages previously mentioned.

Depending on the terms of the IC Agreement, it is estimated that a corporation (SR) can increase payments to you by between 25%-40% because of the cost savings. A cost analysis that will provide details of the corporation's cost savings of switching to a dual hat operation can be easily done by a good accountant.

CHAPTER 15

REQUIREMENTS FOR INDEPENDENT CONTRACTOR STATUS

The simplified requirements stated in Chapter 6, *supra* always remain the same.

APPENDIX

PART V

FORMS, INSTRUCTIONS AND OTHER HELPFUL ITEMS

CHAPTER 16

LAW

There is so much law on the subject of independent contractors that a whole warehouse would be necessary to contain it. FloA has the legal experts in this field and, therefore, we present only the single most important case ever decided on the IC issue.

Smoky Mountain Secrets, Inc. v. U.S., 910 F. Supp. 1316 (E.D. Tenn., 1995) is what lawyers call a seminal case on the IC issue. It provides the protection (through the use of IC Specialists) to guaranty that you are acting properly under the law. The following excerpts show how far we have come in the battle to win work freedom:

"Mr. Gee is a CPA who has been licensed and in practice for more than 20 years. He received his undergraduate degree in accounting from Western Kentucky University and a masters in Business Administration from the University of Tennessee at Knoxville."

*   *   *

"...Mr. Gee opined that SMS's telemarketers and delivery persons were direct sellers as contemplated by (the law). Mr. Gee testified that his opinion was based upon (his client's) description of the relevant facts about SMS's business, the manner in which the telemarketers and delivery persons would be compensated, and the fact that plaintiff had a written contract with its sales force providing that the telemarketers and delivery persons would not be treated as employees for federal tax purposes."

* * *

"Like Mr. Gee, Mr. Sharpe (a CPA) advised (his client) that he believed that SMS's telemarketers and delivery persons were properly classified as independent contractors and not employees. He based this advice, however, upon his prior experience and knowledge of common law (20 common law factors)."

* * *

"After again analyzing SMS's sales force to the context of these 20 factors, Mr. Sharpe advised (his client) that the telemarketers and delivery persons were properly characterized as independent contractors."

* * *

Thus, the only remaining question is whether SMS had a reasonable basis for treating its telemarketers and delivery persons as independent contractors. The term 'reasonable basis' is to be construed liberally in favor of the taxpayer. (Citing authority).

* * *

SMS claims that its reliance on the advice of two advisors is sufficient to demonstrate a reasonable basis under Sec.530 (the Safe Harbor) for not treating its telemarketers and delivery persons as employees. I agree.

Under the circumstances of this case, reliance upon the professional advice rendered by two CPA's...constitutes a reasonable basis for SMS having treated its telemarketers and delivery persons as independent contractors.

*   *   *

"I further conclude that SMS's reliance upon the advice of Mr. Sharpe, who examined the information provided by (his client) in the context of the common law factors governing independent contractor status, was reasonable, thereby entitling SMS to the protection of Sec. 530."

*   *   *

"Generally, the courts have found that reasonable cause exists where the taxpayer relied on the advice of a trusted attorney or accountant. (Citing authority). Indeed in this regard, the Supreme Court has stated that:"
'When an accountant or attorney advises a taxpayer on a matter of tax law, such as whether a liability exists, it is reasonable for the taxpayer to rely on that advice. Most taxpayers are not competent to discern error in the substantive advice of an accountant or attorney. To require the taxpayer to challenge the attorney, to seek a "second opinion," or try to monitor counsel on the provisions of the Code himself would nullify the very purpose of seeking advice of a presumed expert in the first place. "Ordinary business care and prudence" do not demand such actions."(Citing Supreme Court case)."

CHAPTER 17

BIBLIOGRAPHY AND WEBSITES

Jimmy Moore, *Advancing Into Temp, Contract, and Consulting Jobs* (Writer's Club Press an Imprint of Iuniverse.com (2001).
Robert W. Wood, *Legal Guide to Independent Contractor Status*, (Third Edition, A Panel Publication, Aspen Publishers (2000).
Willie Jackson and Edgar H. Gee, Jr. and Michael J. Knight, *How to Shift the Burden of Proof to the IRS on Independent Contractor Status*, 28 Tax Advisor No. 10, 642 (1997)
Russell A. Hollrah, *Employer's Handbook, Independent Contractor* (Thompson Publishing Group).

 The IRS website has a wealth of information and, if you feel that you need it. Of course it is mostly confusing. There is enough blah, blah, blah to fill your house. We have simplified all the complicated language to the bone. However, if you feel the need, go to **www.irs.gov** and search the words, "independent contractors." We suggest, however, that you ignore the blah, blah and follow the SIMPLE requirements previously stated.

However, there are some necessary forms that can be obtained at the IRS site.

- <u>IRS Form 1099.</u> This is the only form that your SR will provide to the IRS and you, the SP. You may need to file estimated payments. See your tax advisor about this. The 1096 Form (for SR's) accompanies the various 1099's and is just a listing of all the 1099 Forms that you may file.
- <u>SS4-Application for EIN.</u> This is an application for an Employer's Identification Number. It should be used by SR's or SP's who want to start a business can open a bank account, which should be separate from your personal account.
- <u>SS9-Request for Taxpayer ID</u>. The SP's should be asked by your SR to complete and return. It prevents the SR from being penalized by the IRS.

Also, there are many websites that claim to cater to Independent Contractor operations—none of them provide the comprehensive multidisciplinary services that FloA provides. The large numbers of sites do show the popularity of independent contractor treatment. However, they provide complicated instructions and unnecessary scare tactics. A simple search of your favorite search engine under "independent contractor" will provide you with more hits than you can handle. The best of the sites are **www.nolo.com** (which also provides good how to do it information on choosing a business entity and other small business topics). Also, Attorney Urquhart's website **www.workerstatus.com** has a wealth of material. For sales and marketing consulting **www.salesgeneration.com** is the best.

CHAPTER 18

FORMS, INSTRUCTIONS AND WORKSHEETS

INDEPENDENT CONTRACTOR QUESTIONNAIRE
FOR CONSTRUCTION SERVICE PROVIDER

DATE
NAME
BUSINESS NAME   CONTACT
BUSINESS ADDRESS
PHONE   FAX   MOBILE
PAGER
HOME ADDRESS   HOME PHONE
SS#   FEDTAX#
REFERRED BY
ARE YOU PRESENTLY DOING SMALL/MED CONTRACTING JOBS?
HOW MANY HELPERS DO YOU NORMALLY USE?
DO YOU HAVE ACCESS TO ADDITIONAL HELP?

IS SOMEONE AVAILABLE TO ANSWER YOUR PHONE DURING WORKING HOURS?
DO YOU HAVE WORKER'S COMPENSATION INSURANCE?
DO YOU HAVE GENERAL LIABILITY INSURANCE?
DO YOU HAVE TRUGK/AUTO INSURANCE?
WILL YOU DO EMERGENCY REPAIRS OUTSDE OF REGULAR BUSINESS HOURS?
WILL YOU DO REGULAR WORK AT NIGHT OR ON WEBKENDS?
HOW FAR WILL YOU TRAVEL FOR WORK?
WHICH COUNTIES?

TRADE SPECIALTY	OWN OR RENT EQUIPMENT	SKILL LEVEL

DEMOLITION
DEBRIS REMOVAL
CLEANING-STRUCTURE
CLEANING-SOFT
CLEANING—HARD FURN.
CLEANING—CARPET
CLEANING-DRY/PLANT
ROUGH CARPENTRY
FINISH CARPENTRY
PUNCH LIST CARPENTRY
DRYWALL
STUCCO/PLASTER
CABINETS
WINDOWS
ACOUSTIC TILE
PAINT INTERIOR
PAINT EXTERIOR
STRIP AND FINISH

SAND AND FINISH
WALLPAPER
INSULATION
CERAMIC TILE
CARPET INSTALLATION
VINYL INSTALLATION
WOOD FLOOR INSTALLATION
ROOFING
MASONRY
VINYL/ALUM. SIDING/TRIM
GARAGE DOORS
ELECTRICAL
PLUMBING
HEATING/AC

    INDEPENDENT CONTRACTOR INFORMATION FORM

TO:
FROM:
DATE:
IN ORDER FOR US TO UTILIZE YOUR SERVICES AS AN INDEPENDENT CONTRACTOR WE NEED THE FOLLOWING INFORMATION
RETURN TO:

___W-9 FORM (FILL OUT, SIGN AND RETURN)
___COPY OF YOUR LIABILITY INSURANCE COMPANY MAILED FROM YOUR INSURANCE COMPANY
___COPY OF YOUR DRIVERS' LICENSE
___IF YOU EMPLOY ANYONE, A COPY OF YOUR WORKMAN'S COMPENSATION INSURANCE
___BUSINESS CARD
___RECENT ADS IN NEWSPAPER
___SOCIAL SECURITY NUMBER OR FEDERAL I.D. NUMBER
___COPY OF YOUR ARTICLES OF INCORPORATION OR D/B/A.

CERTIFICATE
___ INDEPENDENT CONTRACTOR QUESTIONNAIRE
___ OTHER.
TWO REFERENCES THAT YOU RECENTLY HAVE DONE WORK FOR.
    NAME -   PHONE -
    NAME -   PHONE -
IF YOU HAVE ANY QUESTIONS PLEASE CALL. THANK YOU!

INDEPENDENT CONTRACTOR PRE-HIRE WORKSHEET USED BY A UNIVERSITY

Individual Sole Proprietor Corporation
Social Security Number_____
Federal ID Number_____
Name_____
Name of Company_____
Campus_____
Department_____
If Foreign National—Country_____ Visa Type_____

MULTIPLE RELATIONSHIPS WITH THE UNIVERSITY

1. Is this individual on record as a current employee?
Yes No
If no, is it expected that the University will hire this individual as an employee following the termination of this service?
Yes No
2. Was the individual a University employee any time during the last year and did he or she provide the same or similar services while an employee?
Yes No

IRS CLASSIFICATION FACTORS

Before a worker is hired as an independent contractor, the following checklist *must* be completed to help determine whether an employer/employee relationship exists.

IRS Classification Factors Yes =
Employee
No =
Contractor

Behavioral Control: Right to direct and control details and means by which worker performs services.

1. Instructions. Will the University have the right to give the worker instructions about when, where, and how he or she is to do the job?
2. Training. Will the worker receive training from the University?

Financial Control: Right to direct and control economic aspects of the worker's activities.

3. Significant Investment. Has the worker failed to invest in facilities (such as an office) used to perform services?
4. Payment of Expenses. Will the University pay the worker's business or travel expenses?
5. Services Available. Does the worker not make his or her services available to other employers?
6. Payment by Hour, Week, Month. Will the University pay the worker by the hour, week, or month rather than by commission or by the job?
7. Realization of Profit or Loss. Will the arrangement prevent the worker from realizing a profit or suffering a loss?

Relationship of Parties: Intent of parties concerning status and control of worker.

8. Written Contract. Will a written contract not be executed describing the worker as an independent contractor?
9. Employee Benefits. Will the worker receive any employee benefits?
10. Right to Terminate. Could the University terminate the worker at any time without incurring liability?

11. Regular Business Activity. Is the work to be performed part of the regular business of the University, such as teaching or research?

EVALUATION OF CLASSIFICATION FACTORS

Areas That Support Employee Status Areas That Support Contractor Status (Use separate sheet, if necessary.)

DETERMINATION

Hire worker as an employee

Hire worker as an independent contractor

_____

Department Authorization

Prepared By_____

Date_____

SERVICE PROVIDER INSTRUCTIONS FOR COMPLETING AN IC AGREEMENT

Please provide the following information:

Home addresses.

Social Security #s.

The function(s) each of you performs for the corporation, such as sales, field superintendent, marketing services, office management, etc.

The rate of pay you intend to receive, whether hourly, daily, weekly, biweekly, monthly, piecework, or accomplishment of certain tasks.

The term of the agreement.

How it will work:

You will submit an invoice in the following form to the Service Recipient.

(YOUR LETTERHEAD)

INVOICE #

FOR SERVICES RENDERED

FROM (DATE) TO (DATE) PURSUANT TO AGREEMENT $

(Name)

(Telephone)
Accepting jobs for   Services
Please call for appointment

You will also provide an advertisement in you local paper or bulletin board of your local grocery advertising your services to the public.

INSTRUCTIONS FOR SERVICE RECIPIENTS
Obtain a signed completed checklist for IC's from the SP.

The SP is a task oriented individual; he is restricted by you only to the extent of the proper performance of that task. The hours of his work should not be controlled by you but should relate to the time it takes to do the task. You may provide general instructions as to what the task is but you should not instruct the SP with specific instructions on how to do the task. If the person you are hiring is already one of your employees, you should define the new tasks you will be asking him to do that is different than what he is now doing. Usually attaching the management function to the task presently being performed should suffice.

Pay should be determined after obtaining an analysis of labor costs, which we can provide. Pay is to be negotiated, taking also into consideration the cost of any benefits you want to provide. The entire IC agreement can be negotiated as you and the SP may agree. Pay can be by piece work (the items involved in the task), hourly, weekly, etc. Provision should be made to include discretionary (at your discretion) bonuses (either year end or other) but this is optional. Payment is to be made only upon receipt of the SP's invoice.

After all parties sign the IC agreement, the SP should receive a copy and the original placed in his personnel file.

The only IRS documents necessary for filing are the 1099 year end statements (due by January 31st of each year) and the 1096 summary statement (which is a summary of all the 1099's you file). The SP is given a copy for him to use in completing his tax forms.

Besides whatever costs savings you obtain, you should also benefit from increased productivity and a more pleasurable workplace and workforce.

OUTLINE OF APPROACH BY SR'S TO SP'S FOR ESTABLISHMENT OF AN INDEPENDENT CONTRACTOR RELATIONSHIP

<u>Before interview</u>

Advertise for contractors or service providers.

Use appropriate application form.

<u>During interview</u>—make them feel good about arrangement.

1. Use proper terms (contractor, service provider, representative) vs. employee, job, and salesman.
2. Assume that person knows the difference between an employee and an independent contractor and discuss it from that point of view.
3. Explain that all your workers are contractors (service providers) and they want it that way because the advantages outweigh the disadvantages, especially gross pay and allowance of business deductions—(list others from outline). Allowable expenses are often permitted as a percentage of gross and usually amount to 50% of gross or more. The amount is different for each industry but accountants are aware of the percentage.

At end of year a 1099 form is sent just like a bank does for interest.

4. Payments are made in full with no deductions and can be structured to take care of estimated tax payments, if contractor chooses to make estimated payments. Half of self-employment taxes are now deductible and it is probable in the future that they will be fully deductible.
5. You will assist at end of year to do taxes, if this is new. You have accountants who do other contractors. Also, you will provide assistance in finding appropriate insurance agents for liability, health, disability and pension information.

CHAPTER 19

VARIOUS AGREEMENTS AND OPTIONAL CLAUSES

No form independent contractor agreement can particularize your special needs. FloA can provide detailed specialized IC agreement to suit your needs. What follows are various stock agreements and specialized provisions that should enable you to put your own agreements together but, remember, self-help has its drawbacks and we would be glad to provide drafting help. The following Agreement is the one that FloA uses:

FloA's General Independent Contractor Agreement

AGREEMENT IS HEREBY MADE between the SERVICE RECIPIENT and SERVICE PROVIDER set forth below according to the following terms, conditions, and provisions:

1. IDENTITY OF SERVICE RECIPIENT. Service Recipient is identified as follows:

   Name:

   Type Entity: ( ) Sole Proprietorship ( )Partnership
                ( ) Corporation   ( )Limited Liability Company
                ( ) d/b/a   ( ) Other

   Address:

   City/State/Zip:

   Business—Tele.:   Fax:

2. IDENTITY OF SERVICE PROVIDER. The Service Provider is identified as follows:

   Name:

   Type Entity: ( ) Sole Proprietorship ( )Partnership
                ( ) Corporation   ( )Limited Liability Company
                ( ) d/b/a   ( )Other

   Address:

   City/State/Zip:

   Business—Tele.:   Fax:

   Social Security or Federal I.D. #

3. NATURE OF RELATIONSHIP. The Service Provider is an independent contractor in his relationship with Service Recipient. This means, as follows:

a. Service Recipient has neither the right to nor shall he exercise any control or direction over the methods by which Service Provider performs the duties and functions of Service Provider. Service Provider will devote his best efforts in the performance of his duties as hereafter set forth;
b. Service Provider is an independent businessperson who offers his services to the public at large and has the right to perform services for others during the term of this agreement. Service Provider has the sole right to control and direct the means, manner and method by which the services required by this agreement will be performed. Service Provider has the right to perform the services required by this agreement at any agreeable location and the time spent by Service Provider is solely at his/her discretion within any monetary caps which are agreeable to both parties;
c. Service Provider owns or rents the tools used in performance of his services to Service Recipient;
d. Service Provider is responsible for payment of his own taxes and shall make no claim against Service Recipient for pension benefits, liability insurance, or medical insurance, other than as may hereafter be stated in this contract;
e. Service Provider is responsible for his own negligence and hereby specifically holds Service Recipient harmless and agrees to defend and indemnify ServiceRecipient.
f. Service Recipient shall not be liable to Service Provider for any expenses paid or incurred by Service Provider unless otherwise agreed in writing.
g. Service Provider shall supply, at Service Provider's sole expense, all equipment, tools, materials, and/or supplies to accomplish the job agreed to be performed.
h. Neither federal, nor state, nor local income tax, nor payroll tax of any kind shall be withheld or paid by Service Recipient on behalf of Service Provider or the employees of Service Provider. Service

Provider shall not be treated as an employee with respect to the services performed hereunder for federal or state tax purposes.

i. Service Provider understands that Service Provider is responsible to pay, according to law, Service Provider's income tax. If Service Provider is not a corporation, Service Provider further understands that Service Provider may be liable for self-employment (social security) tax, to be paid by Service Provider according to law.

j. Because Service Provider is engaged in Service Provider's own independently established business, Service Provider is not eligible for, and shall not participate in, any employee pension, health, or other fringe benefit plan, of the Service Recipient.

k. No workers' compensation insurance shall be obtained by Service Recipient concerning Service Provider or the employees of Service Provider. Service Provider shall comply with the workers' compensation law concerning Service Provider and the employees of Service Provider .

l. Service Recipient is not responsible for Unemployment Compensation and will not pay any Federal Unemployment Tax on behalf of Service Provider and Service Provider expressly waives and releases Service Recipient for any responsibility for same and Service Provider hereby states that it will make no claim for such benefits.

m. Service Provider warrants that he has entered into this agreement with full knowledge and understanding of its terms freely and voluntarily.

4. PROJECTS TO BE PERFORMED. Service Recipient desires that Service Provider perform and Service Provider agrees to perform the following project(s):

5. TERMS OF PAYMENT. Service Recipient will pay a fee of $
(Terms of Payments)

Service Recipient shall pay Service Provider 's fee within a reasonable time after receiving Service Provider 's invoice. Invoices shall be submitted on Service Provider's letterhead specifying: (i) an invoice number, (ii) the dates covered in the invoice, (iii) an outline of the work performed during the period.

6. TERM OF AGREEMENT. The period within which the Service Provider services are to be rendered under this Agreement shall commence on   and shall, at the latest terminate on, but may be renewed for the same additional term if agreed to by both parties.

7. TERMINATION WITHOUT CAUSE. Without cause, either party may terminate this agreement after giving 15 days prior written notice to the other of intent to terminate without cause. The parties shall deal with each other in good faith during the 15-day period after any notice of intent to terminate without cause has been given.

8. TERMINATION WITH CAUSE. With reasonable cause, either party may terminate this agreement effective immediately upon the giving of notice of termination for cause. Reasonable cause shall include:
 A. Material violation of this agreement.
 B. Any act exposing the other party to liability to others for personal injury or property damage.
 C. Unacceptable quality of work.

9. NON-WAIVER. The failure of either party to exercise any of its rights under this agreement for a breach thereof shall not be deemed to be a waiver of such rights or a waiver of any subsequent breach.

10. NO AUTHORITY TO BIND SERVICE RECIPIENT . Service Provider has no authority to enter into contracts or agreements on behalf

of Service Recipient. This agreement does not create a partnership or agency relationship between the parties.

11. DECLARATION BY SERVICE PROVIDER. Service Provider declares that Service Provider has complied with all federal, state and local laws regarding business permits, certificates and licenses that may be required to carry out the work to be performed under this agreement.

12. HOW NOTICES SHALL BE GIVEN. Any written notice given in connection with this agreement shall be given in writing and shall be delivered either by hand or by certified mail, return receipt requested, to the party at the party's address stated herein. Any party may change its address stated herein by giving notice of the change in accordance with this paragraph.

13. ASSIGNABILITY. This agreement may not be assigned, in whole or in part, by Service Provider.

14. CHOICE OF LAW. Any dispute under this agreement or related to this agreement shall be decided in accordance with the laws of the State of.

15. ARBITRATION. Any dispute which may arise between the parties shall be submitted to binding arbitration. Each party shall select an Arbitrator and the two Arbitrators shall select a third. The decision of the Arbitrators shall be binding and final and shall be subject to enforcement in a Court action. Prior to any arbitration decision, costs of arbitration shall be divided equally by the parties.

16. ENTIRE AGREEMENT. This is the entire agreement of the parties.

17. SEVERABILITY. If any part of this agreement shall be held unenforceable, the rest of this agreement will nevertheless remain in full force and effect.

18. AMENDMENTS. This agreement may be supplemented, amended or revised only in writing by agreement of the parties.

19. ATTORNEY'S FEES. If any legal action or arbitration or other proceeding is brought for the enforcement of the Agreement, or because of an alleged dispute, breach, default, or misrepresentation in connection with any of the provisions of the Agreement, the successful or prevailing party shall be entitled to recover reasonable attorneys' fees and other costs incurred in that action or proceeding, in addition to any other relief to which they may be entitled.

AGREED:
Dated:

_____
, Service Recipient

_____
, Service Provider

Independent Contractor Agreement for Household Workers

This Agreement is made between _____ (Client) with a principal place of business at _____ and _____ (Contractor), with a principal place of business at: _____.
This Agreement will become effective on _____, _____ and will end no later than _____, _____.
Services to be performed

Contractor agrees to perform the following services.
a. Cleaning Interior
Contractor will clean the following rooms and areas: _____
_____
_____

b. Cleaning Exterior
Contractor will clean the following:
__ Front porch or deck: _____
__ Back porch or deck: _____
__ Garage: _____
__ Pool, hot tub or sauna: _____
__ Other exterior areas: _____

c. Gardening
Contractor will perform the following gardening services: _____
_____
_____

d. Other Responsibilities
__ Cooking: _____
__ Laundry: _____
__ Ironing: _____
__ Shopping and errands: _____
__ Other: _____

Payment

In consideration for the services to be performed by Contractor, Client agrees to pay Contractor at the rate of $_____ per [Circle one: hour, day, week, month] according to the terms of payment set forth below.

Terms of Payment

Upon completing Contractor's services under this Agreement, Contractor shall submit an invoice. Client shall pay Contractor the compensation described within a reasonable time after receiving Contractor's invoice.

Expenses

Contractor shall be responsible for all expenses incurred while performing services under this Agreement. This includes license fees, memberships and dues; automobile and other travel expenses; meals and entertainment; insurance premiums; and all salary, expenses and other compensation paid to employees or contract personnel the Contractor hires to complete the work under this Agreement.

Independent Contractor Status

Contractor is an independent contractor, not Client's employee. Contractor's employees or contract personnel are not Client's employees. Contractor and Client agree to the following rights consistent with an independent contractor relationship.

* Contractor has the right to perform services for others during the term of this Agreement.
* Contractor has the sole right to control and direct the means, manner and method by which the services required by this Agreement will be performed.
* Contractor has the right to perform the services required by this Agreement at any place, location or time.
* Contractor will furnish all equipment and materials used to provide the services required by this Agreement except for _____ _____.
* Contractor has the right to hire assistants as subcontractors, or to use employees to provide the services required by this Agreement.
* The Contractor or Contractor's employees or contract personnel shall perform the services required by this Agreement; Client shall not hire, supervise or pay any assistants to help Contractor.
* Neither Contractor nor Contractor's employees or contract personnel shall receive any training from Client in the skills necessary to perform the services required by this Agreement.
* Client shall not require Contractor or Contractor's employees or contract personnel to devote full time to performing the services required by this Agreement.

Time and Place of Performance
Contractor shall perform the services at _____
_____
____ during reasonable hours on a schedule to be mutually agreed upon by Client and Contractor based upon Client's needs and Contractor's availability to perform such services.

Business Permits, Certificates and Licenses
Contractor has complied with all federal, state and local laws requiring business permits, certificates and licenses required to carry out the services to be performed under this Agreement.

State and Federal Taxes
Client will not:
* withhold FICA (Social Security and Medicare taxes) from Contractor's payments or make FICA payments on Contractor's behalf
* make state or federal unemployment compensation contributions on Contractor's behalf, or
* withhold state or federal income tax from Contractor's payments.

Contractor shall pay all taxes incurred while performing services under this Agreement—including all applicable income taxes and, if Contractor is not a corporation, self-employment (Social Security) taxes. Upon demand, Contractor shall provide Client with proof that such payments have been made.

Workers' Compensation
Client shall not obtain workers' compensation insurance on behalf of Contractor or Contractor's employees. If Contractor hires employees to perform any work under this Agreement, Contractor will cover them with workers' compensation insurance and provide Client with a certificate of workers' compensation insurance before the employees begin the work.

Unemployment Compensation
Client shall make no state or federal unemployment compensation payments on behalf of Contractor or Contractor's employees or contract

personnel. Contractor will not be entitled to these benefits in connection with work performed under this Agreement.

Terminating the Agreement
(Check applicable provision.)

____ With reasonable cause, either Client or Contractor may terminate this Agreement, effective immediately upon giving written notice. Reasonable cause includes:
- * a material violation of this Agreement, or
- * any act exposing the other party to liability to others for personal injury or property damage.

OR

____ Either party may terminate this Agreement any time by giving thirty days written notice to the other party of the intent to terminate.

Signatures

Client:

Name of Client: _____

By: _____
     (Signature)

_____
(Typed or Printed Name)

Title: _____

Date: _____

Contractor:

Name of Contractor: _____

By: _____
     (Signature)

_____
(Typed or Printed Name)

Taxpayer ID Number: _____

Date: _____

Independent Contractor Agreement for Real Estate Salesperson

This Agreement is made between _____ (Broker) with a principal place of business at _____ and _____ (Salesperson), with a principal place of business at: _____.

Services to be Performed

Salesperson agrees to sell, lease or rent real estate listed with Broker. Salesperson will not be treated as an employee with respect to the services performed by salesperson as a real estate agent for federal tax purposes.

Compensation

In consideration for the services to be performed by Salesperson, Broker agrees to pay Salesperson a commission on completed sales by Salesperson as follows: _____.

Salesperson shall have no right to compensation based on the number of hours worked.

Expenses

Salesperson shall be responsible for all expenses incurred while performing services under this Agreement. This includes license fees, memberships and dues; automobile and other travel expenses; meals and entertainment; insurance premiums; and all salary, expenses and other compensation paid to employees or contract personnel the Salesperson hires to complete the work under this Agreement.

Broker's Sales Office

Broker agrees to provide Salesperson with the use, equally with other Salespersons, of all the facilities of the sales office operated by Broker at _____ [address of Broker's real estate office to be used by salesperson].

Independent Contractor Status
Salesperson is an independent contractor, not Broker's employee. Salesperson's employees or contract personnel are not Broker's employees. Salesperson and Broker agree to the following rights consistent with an independent contractor relationship.

* Salesperson has the right to perform services for others during the term of this Agreement.
* Salesperson has the sole right to control and direct the means, manner and method by which the services required by this Agreement will be performed.
* Subject to any restrictions on Contractor's sales territory contained in this Agreement, Salesperson has the right to perform the services required by this Agreement at any location or time.
* Salesperson has the right to hire assistants as subcontractors, or to use employees to provide the services required by this Agreement.

Business Permits, Certificates and Licenses

Salesperson has complied with all federal, state and local laws requiring business permits, certificates and licenses required to carry out the services to be performed under this Agreement.

Salesperson represents and warrants that Salesperson is a licensed real estate salesperson in good standing, having been licensed by _____ _____ on _____ [date].

State and Federal Taxes

Broker will not:
* withhold FICA (Social Security and Medicare taxes) from Salesperson's payments or make FICA payments on Salesperson's behalf
* make state or federal unemployment compensation contributions on Salesperson's behalf, or
* withhold state or federal income tax from Salesperson's payments.

Salesperson shall pay all taxes incurred while performing services under this Agreement including all applicable income taxes and, if Salesperson is not a corporation, self-employment (Social Security) taxes. Upon demand, Salesperson shall provide Broker with proof that such payments have been made.

Fringe Benefits

Salesperson understands that neither Salesperson nor Salesperson's employees or contract personnel are eligible to participate in any employee pension, health, vacation pay, sick pay or other fringe benefit plan of Broker.

Workers' Compensation

Broker shall not obtain workers' compensation insurance on behalf of Salesperson or Salesperson's employees. If Salesperson hires employees to perform any work under this Agreement, Salesperson will cover them with workers' compensation insurance to the extent required by law and provide Broker with a certificate of workers' compensation insurance before the employees begin the work.

Optional Language

Salesperson shall obtain workers' compensation insurance coverage for Salesperson. Salesperson shall provide Broker with proof that such coverage has been obtained before starting work.

Unemployment Compensation

Broker shall make no state or federal unemployment compensation payments on behalf of Salesperson or Salesperson's employees or contract personnel. Salesperson will not be entitled to these benefits in connection with work performed under this Agreement.

Insurance

Broker shall not provide any insurance coverage of any kind for Salesperson or Salesperson's employees or contract personnel. Salesperson agrees to maintain an insurance policy in an adequate amount to cover any negligent acts committed by Salesperson or Salesperson's employees or agents while performing services under this Agreement.

Salesperson shall indemnify and hold Broker harmless from any loss or liability arising from performing services under this Agreement.

This includes any claim for injuries or damages caused by Salesperson while traveling in Salesperson's automobile and performing services under this Agreement.

Terminating the Agreement

With reasonable cause, either Broker or Salesperson may terminate this Agreement, effective immediately upon giving written notice.

Reasonable cause includes:
* a material violation of this Agreement, or
* any act exposing the other party to liability to others for personal injury or property damage.

OR

Either party may terminate this Agreement any time by giving thirty days written notice to the other party of the intent to terminate.

Exclusive Agreement

This is the entire Agreement between Salesperson and Broker.

Resolving Disputes

If a dispute arises under this Agreement, any party may take the matter to court.

Additional Option

If any court action is necessary to enforce this Agreement, the prevailing party shall be entitled to reasonable attorney fees, costs and expenses in addition to any other relief to which he or she may be entitled.

OR

If a dispute arises under this Agreement, the parties agree to first try to resolve the dispute with the help of a mutually agreed-upon mediator in _____. Any costs and fees other than attorney fees associated with the mediation shall be shared equally by the parties.

If the dispute is not resolved within 30 days after it is referred to the mediator, any party may take the matter to court.

Additional Option

If any court action is necessary to enforce this Agreement, the prevailing party shall be entitled to reasonable attorney fees, costs and expenses in addition to any other relief to which he or she may be entitled.

OR

If a dispute arises under this Agreement, the parties agree to first try to resolve the dispute with the help of a mutually agreed-upon mediator in _____. Any costs and fees other than attorney fees associated with the mediation shall be shared equally by the parties.

If it proves impossible to arrive at a mutually satisfactory solution through mediation, the parties agree to submit the dispute to a mutually agreed upon arbitrator in _____. Judgment upon the award rendered by the arbitrator may be entered in any court having jurisdiction to do so. Costs of arbitration, including attorney fees, will be allocated by the arbitrator.

Applicable Law

This Agreement will be governed by the laws of the State of _____ _____.

Notices

All notices and other communications in connection with this Agreement shall be in writing and shall be considered given as follows:
- * when delivered personally to the recipient's address as stated on this Agreement
- * three days after being deposited in the United States mail, with postage prepaid to the recipient's address as stated on this Agreement, or
- * when sent by fax or telex to the last fax or telex number of the recipient known to the person giving notice. Notice is effective upon receipt provided that a duplicate copy of the notice is promptly given by first class mail, or the recipient delivers a written confirmation of receipt.

No Partnership

This Agreement does not create a partnership relationship. Salesperson does not have authority to enter into contracts on Broker's behalf.

Signatures

Client:
Name of Client: _____
By: _____
   (Signature)
_____
   (Typed or Printed Name)
Title: _____
Date: _____

Contractor:
Name of Salesperson: _____

By: _____
   (Signature)

_____
   (Typed or Printed Name)
Taxpayer ID Number: _____
Date: _____

Independent Contractor Agreement for Construction Contractor

This Agreement is made between _____ ("Owner"), with a principal place of business at _____, and _____ ("Contractor"), with a principal place of business at _____.

1. Services to Be Performed

Contractor shall furnish all labor and materials to construct and complete the project shown on the contract documents contained in Exhibit A, which is attached to and made part of this Agreement.

2. Payment

(Check and complete applicable provision.)

[ ] Owner shall pay Contractor for all labor and materials the sum of $ _____.

OR:

[ ] Owner shall pay Contractor $ _____ for labor. Materials shall be paid for by Owner upon delivery to the worksite, or as follows: _____.

3. Terms of Payment

(Check and complete applicable provision.)

[ ] Upon completing Contractor's services under this Agreement, Contractor shall submit an invoice. Owner shall pay Contractor within _____ days from the date of Contractor's invoice.

OR:

[ ] Contractor shall be paid $ _____ upon signing this Agreement and the remaining amount due when Contractor completes the services and submits an invoice. Owner shall pay Contractor within _____ days from the date of Contractor's invoice.

OR:

[ ] Contractor shall be paid according to the Schedule of Payments set forth in Exhibit attached to and made part of this agreement.

(Optional: Check and complete if applicable.)

[ ] 4. Late Fees

Late payments by Owner shall be subject to late penalty fees of _____ % per month from the due date until the amount is paid.

5. Time of Completion

The work to be performed under this Agreement shall commence on _____ and be substantially completed on or before _____.

6. Permits and Approvals

(Check applicable provision.)

[ ] Owner shall be responsible for determining which state and local permits are necessary for performing the specified work, and for obtaining and paying for the permits.

OR:

[ ] Contractor shall be responsible for determining which state and local permits are necessary for performing the specified work, and for obtaining and paying for the permits.

7. Limited Warranty

Contractor warrants that all work shall be completed in a good workmanlike manner and in compliance with all building codes and other applicable laws.

8. Site Maintenance

Contractor agrees to be bound by the following conditions when performing the specified work:

- Contractor shall remove all debris and leave the premises in a broom clean condition.
- Contractor shall perform the specified work during the following hours: _____
- Contractor agrees that disruptively loud activities shall be performed only at the following times: _____.

- At the end of each day's work, Contractor's equipment shall be stored in the following location: _____.

9. Subcontractors

Contractor may at its discretion engage subcontractors to perform services under this Agreement, but Contractor shall remain responsible for proper completion of this Agreement.

10. Independent Contractor Status

Contractor is an independent contractor, not Owner's employee. Contractor's employees or subcontractors are not Owner's employees. Contractor and Owner agree to the following rights consistent with an independent contractor relationship.

- Contractor has the right to perform services for others during the term of this Agreement.
- Contractor has the sole right to control and direct the means, manner and method by which the services required by this Agreement will be performed.
- The Contractor or Contractor's employees or subcontractors shall perform the services required by this Agreement; Owner shall not hire, supervise or pay any assistants to help Contractor.
- Owner shall not require Contractor or Contractor's employees or subcontractors to devote full time to performing the services required by this Agreement.
- Neither Contractor nor Contractor's employees or subcontractors are eligible to participate in any employee pension, health, vacation pay, sick pay or other fringe benefit plan of Owner.

11. Local, State and Federal Taxes

Contractor shall pay all income taxes, and FICA (Social Security and Medicare taxes) incurred while performing services under this Agreement. Owner will not:

- withhold FICA from Contractor's payments or make FICA payments on Contractor's behalf

- make state or federal unemployment compensation contributions on Contractor's behalf, or
- withhold state or federal income tax from Contractor's payments.

The charges included here do not include taxes. If Contractor is required to pay any federal, state or local sales, use, property or value added taxes based on the services provided under this Agreement, the taxes shall be separately billed to Owner. Contractor shall not pay any interest or penalties incurred due to late payment or nonpayment of any taxes by Owner.

12. Insurance

Contractor agrees to obtain adequate business liability insurance for injuries to its employees and others incurring loss or injury as a result of the acts of Contractor or its employees or subcontractors.

13. Terminating the Agreement

(Check and complete applicable provision.)

[ ] With reasonable cause, either Owner or Contractor may terminate this Agreement effective immediately by giving written notice of cause for termination. Reasonable cause includes:
- a material violation of this Agreement, or
- nonpayment of Contractor's compensation after 20 days written demand for payment.

Contractor shall be entitled to full payment for services performed prior to the effective date of termination.

OR:

[ ] Either Owner or Contractor may terminate this Agreement at any time by giving day's written notice of termination. Contractor shall be entitled to full payment for services performed prior to the date of termination.

14. Exclusive Agreement

This is the entire Agreement between Contractor and Owner.

(Optional: Check if applicable.)

[ ] 15. Modifying the Agreement

Owner and Contractor recognize that:

- Contractor's original cost and time estimates may be too low due to unforeseen events, or to factors unknown to Contractor when this Agreement was made
- Owner may desire a mid-project change in Contractor's services that would add time and cost to the project and possibly inconvenience Contractor, or
- Other provisions of this Agreement may be difficult to carry out due to unforeseen circumstances.

If any intended changes or any other events beyond the parties' control require adjustments to this Agreement, the parties shall make a good faith effort to agree on all necessary particulars. Such agreements shall be put in writing, signed by the parties and added to this Agreement.

16. Resolving Disputes

(Choose Alternative A, B or C and any desired optional clauses.)

    Alternative A

[ ] If a dispute arises under this Agreement, any party may take the matter to court.

(Optional: Check if applicable.)

[ ] If any court action is necessary to enforce this Agreement, the prevailing party shall be entitled to reasonable attorney fees, costs and expenses in addition to any other relief to which he or she may be entitled.

    Alternative B

[ ] If a dispute arises under this Agreement, the parties agree to first try to resolve the dispute with the help of a mutually agreed-upon mediator in _____ [List city or county where mediation will occur]. Any costs and fees other than attorney fees associated with the mediation shall be shared equally by the parties. If the dispute is not resolved within 30 days after it is referred to the mediator, any party may take the matter to court.

(Optional: Check if applicable.)

[ ] If any court action is necessary to enforce this Agreement, the prevailing party shall be entitled to reasonable attorney fees, costs and expenses in addition to any other relief to which he or she may be entitled.

Alternative C

[ ] If a dispute arises under this Agreement, the parties agree to first try to resolve the dispute with the help of a mutually agreed-upon mediator in _____ [List city or county where mediation will occur]. Any costs and fees other than attorney fees associated with the mediation shall be shared equally by the parties. If it proves impossible to arrive at a mutually satisfactory solution through mediation, the parties agree to submit the dispute to a mutually agreed-upon arbitrator in _____ [List city or county where arbitration will occur]. Judgment upon the award rendered by the arbitrator may be entered in any court having jurisdiction to do so. Costs of arbitration, including attorney fees, will be allocated by the arbitrator.

17. Notices

All notices and other communications in connection with this Agreement shall be in writing and shall be considered given as follows:

- when delivered personally to the recipient's address as stated on this Agreement.
- three days after being deposited in the United States mail, with postage prepaid to the recipient's address as stated on this Agreement, or
- when sent by fax or telex to the last fax or telex number of the recipient known to the person giving notice. Notice is effective upon receipt provided that a duplicate copy of the notice is promptly given by first class mail, or the recipient delivers a written confirmation of receipt.

18. No Partnership

This Agreement does not create a partnership relationship. Neither party has authority to enter into contracts on the other's behalf.

19. Applicable Law
This Agreement will be governed by the laws of the State of _____
_____.
Signatures
Owner:
_____ {Name of Owner
By: _____
   Signature
_____ [Typed or Printed Name]
Title: _____
Date: _____
Contractor:
_____ [Name of Contractor]
By: _____
   Signature
_____ [Typed or Printed Name]
Title: _____
Taxpayer ID Number: _____
Date: _____

Independent Contractor Agreement for Creative Contractor

This Agreement is made between _____ ("Client"), with a principal place of business at _____, and _____ ("Contractor"), with a principal place of business at _____.

1. Services to be Performed
(Check and complete applicable provision.)
[ ] Contractor agrees to perform the following services on Client's behalf:
_____

OR:

[ ] Contractor agrees to perform the services described in Exhibit A, which is attached to this Agreement.

2. Payment

(Check and complete applicable provision.)

[ ] In consideration for the services to be performed by Contractor, Client agrees to pay Contractor $ _____.

OR:

[ ] In consideration for the services to be performed by Contractor, Client agrees to pay Contractor at the rate of $ _____ per _____ [hour, day, week or other unit of time].

(Optional: Check and complete if applicable.)

[ ] Contractor's total compensation shall not exceed $ _____ without Client's written consent.

3. Terms of Payment

(Check and complete applicable provision.)

[ ] Upon completing Contractor's services under this Agreement, Contractor shall submit an invoice. Client shall pay Contractor within _____ days from the date of Contractor's invoice.

OR:

[ ] Contractor shall be paid $ _____ upon signing this Agreement and the remaining amount due when Contractor completes the services and submits an invoice. Client shall pay Contractor within _____ days from the date of Contractor's invoice.

OR:

[ ] Contractor shall be paid according to the Schedule of Payments set forth in Exhibit attached to and made part of this Agreement.

OR:

[ ] Contractor shall send Client an invoice monthly. Client shall pay Contractor within _____ days from the date of each invoice.

(Optional: Check and complete if applicable.)

[ ] 4. Late Fees

Late payments by Client shall be subject to late penalty fees of _____ % per month from the due date until the amount is paid.

5. Expenses

(Check and complete applicable provision)

Alternative A

[ ] Contractor shall be responsible for all expenses incurred while performing services under this Agreement.

(Optional: Check if applicable.)

[ ] However, Client shall reimburse Contractor for all reasonable travel and living expenses necessarily incurred by Contractor while away from Contractor's regular place of business to perform services under this Agreement. Contractor shall submit an itemized statement of such expenses. Client shall pay Contractor within 30 days from the date of each statement.

OR:

Alternative B

[ ] Client shall reimburse Contractor for the following expenses that are directly attributable to work performed under this Agreement:

- travel expenses other than normal commuting, including airfares, rental vehicles and highway mileage in company or personal vehicles at __ cents per mile
- telephone, fax, online and telegraph charges
- postage and courier services
- printing and reproduction
- computer services, and
- other expenses resulting from the work performed under this Agreement.

Contractor shall submit an itemized statement of Contractor's expenses. Client shall pay Contractor within 30 days from the date of each statement.

6. Materials

Contractor will furnish all materials and equipment used to provide the services required by this Agreement.

7. Intellectual Property Ownership

(Check and complete applicable provision.)

ALTERNATIVE A

[ ] Contractor hereby licenses to Client the following intellectual property rights in the work created or developed by Contractor under this Agreement: _____.

This license is conditioned upon full payment of the compensation due Contractor under this Agreement. Contractor reserves all rights not expressly granted to Client by this Agreement.

(Check applicable provision.)

[ ] The rights granted above are exclusive to Client.

OR:

[ ] The rights granted above are nonexclusive.

OR:

ALTERNATIVE B

[ ] Contractor assigns to Client all patent, copyright and trade secret rights in anything created or developed by Contractor for Client under this Agreement. This assignment is conditioned upon full payment of the compensation due Contractor under this Agreement.

Contractor shall help prepare any documents Client considers necessary to secure any copyright, patent or other intellectual property rights at no charge to Client. However, Client shall reimburse Contractor for reasonable out-of-pocket expenses..

(Optional: Check if applicable.)

[ ] 8. Reusable Materials

Contractor owns or holds a license to use and sublicense various materials in existence before the start date of this Agreement (Contractor's Materials). Contractor's Materials include, but are not limited to, those items identified in Exhibit _____, attached to and made part of this Agreement. Contractor may, at its option, include Contractor's Materials in the work performed under this Agreement. Contractor retains all right, title and interest, including all copyrights, patent rights and trade secret rights in Contractor's Materials. Contractor grants Client a royalty-free nonexclusive license to use any Contractor's Materials incorporated into the work performed by Contractor under this Agreement. The license shall have a perpetual term and may not be transferred by Client.

9. Releases

Client shall obtain all necessary copyright permissions and privacy releases for materials included in the Designs at Client's request. Client shall indemnify Contractor against all claims and expenses, including reasonable attorney fees, due to Client's failure to obtain such permissions or releases.

10. Copyright Notice and Credit Line

A copyright notice and credit line in Contractor's name shall accompany any reproduction of the Designs in the following form: _____

_____

11. Term of Agreement

This agreement will become effective when signed by both parties and will terminate on the earlier of:

- the date Contractor completes the services required by this Agreement
- _____ [date], or
- the date a party terminates the Agreement as provided below.

12. Terminating the Agreement

(Check and complete applicable provision.)

[ ] With reasonable cause, either party may terminate this Agreement effective immediately by giving written notice of termination for cause. Reasonable cause includes:

- a material violation of this Agreement, or
- nonpayment of Contractor's compensation after 20 days written demand for payment.

Contractor shall be entitled to full payment for services performed prior to the effective date of termination.

OR:

[ ] Either party may terminate this Agreement at any time by giving _____ days written notice of termination. Contractor shall be entitled to full payment for services performed prior to the date of termination.

13. Independent Contractor Status

Contractor is an independent contractor, not Client's employee. Contractor's employees or subcontractors are not Client's employees. Contractor and Client agree to the following rights consistent with an independent contractor relationship.

- Contractor has the right to perform services for others during the term of this Agreement.
- Contractor has the sole right to control and direct the means, manner and method by which the services required by this Agreement will be performed.
- Contractor has the right to hire assistants as subcontractors, or to use employees to provide the services required by this Agreement.
- Contractor or Contractor's employees or subcontractors shall perform the services required by this Agreement; Client shall not hire, supervise or pay any assistants to help Contractor.
- Neither Contractor nor Contractor's employees or subcontractors shall receive any training from Client in the skills necessary to perform the services required by this Agreement.
- Client shall not require Contractor or Contractor's employees or subcontractors to devote full time to performing the services required by this Agreement.
- Neither Contractor nor Contractor's employees or subcontractors are eligible to participate in any employee pension, health, vacation pay, sick pay or other fringe benefit plan of Client.

14. Local, State and Federal Taxes

Contractor shall pay all income taxes and FICA (Social Security and Medicare taxes) incurred while performing services under this Agreement. Client will not:

- withhold FICA from Contractor's payments or make FICA payments on Contractor's behalf
- make state or federal unemployment compensation contributions on Contractor's behalf, or
- withhold state or federal income tax from Contractor's payments.

The charges included here do not include taxes. If Contractor is required to pay any federal, state or local sales, use, property or value added taxes based on the services provided under this Agreement, the taxes shall be separately billed to Client. Contractor shall not pay any interest or penalties incurred due to late payment or nonpayment of any taxes by Client.

15. Exclusive Agreement

This is the entire Agreement between Contractor and Client.
(Optional: Check if applicable.)

[ ] 16. Modifying the Agreement

Client and Contractor recognize that:
- Contractor's original cost and time estimates may be too low due to unforeseen events, or to factors unknown to Contractor when this Agreement was made
- Client may desire a mid-project change in Contractor's services that would add time and cost to the project and possibly inconvenience Contractor, or
- Other provisions of this Agreement may be difficult to carry out due to unforeseen circumstances.

If any intended changes or any other events beyond the parties' control require adjustments to this Agreement, the parties shall make a good faith effort to agree on all necessary particulars. Such agreements shall be put in writing, signed by the parties and added to this Agreement.

17. Resolving Disputes

(Choose Alternative A, B or C and any desired optional clauses.)

Alternative A

[ ] If a dispute arises under this Agreement, any party may take the matter to court.

(Optional: Check if applicable.)
[ ] If any court action is necessary to enforce this Agreement, the prevailing party shall be entitled to reasonable attorney fees, costs and expenses in addition to any other relief to which he or she may be entitled.

Alternative B

[ ] If a dispute arises under this Agreement, the parties agree to first try to resolve the dispute with the help of a mutually agreed-upon mediator in _____ [List city or county where mediation will occur]. Any costs and fees other than attorney fees associated with the mediation shall be shared equally by the parties. If the dispute is not resolved within 30 days after it is referred to the mediator, any party may take the matter to court.

[ ] (Optional: Check if applicable.) If any court action is necessary to enforce this Agreement, the prevailing party shall be entitled to reasonable attorney fees, costs and expenses in addition to any other relief to which he or she may be entitled.

Alternative C

[ ] If a dispute arises under this Agreement, the parties agree to first try to resolve the dispute with the help of a mutually agreed-upon mediator in _____ [List city or county where mediation will occur]. Any costs and fees other than attorney fees associated with the mediation shall be shared equally by the parties. If it proves impossible to arrive at a mutually satisfactory solution through mediation, the parties agree to submit the dispute to a mutually agreed-upon arbitrator in _____ [List city or county where arbitration will occur]. Judgment upon the award rendered by the arbitrator may be entered in any court having jurisdiction to do so. Costs of arbitration, including attorney fees, will be allocated by the arbitrator.

[ ] 18. (Optional: Check and complete if applicable.) Limited Liability
This provision allocates the risks under this Agreement between Contractor and Client. Contractor's pricing reflects the allocation of risk and limitation of liability specified below.

Contractor's total liability to Client under this Agreement for damages, costs and expenses shall not exceed $ _____ or the compensation received by Contractor under this Agreement, whichever is less.

However, contractor shall remain liable for bodily injury or personal property damage resulting from grossly negligent or willful actions of Contractor, or Contractor's employees or agents while on Client's premises to the extent such actions or omissions were not caused by Client.

NEITHER PARTY TO THIS AGREEMENT SHALL BE LIABLE FOR THE OTHER'S LOST PROFITS, OR SPECIAL, INCIDENTAL OR CONSEQUENTIAL DAMAGES, WHETHER IN AN ACTION IN CONTRACT OR TORT, EVEN IF THE PARTY HAS BEEN HAS BEEN ADVISED BY THE OTHER PARTY OF THE POSSIBILITY OF SUCH DAMAGES.

19. Notices

All notices and other communications in connection with this Agreement shall be in writing and shall be considered given as follows:

- when delivered personally to the recipient's address as stated on this Agreement
- three days after being deposited in the United States mail, with postage prepaid to the recipient's address as stated on this Agreement, or
- when sent by fax or telex to the last fax or telex number of the recipient known to the person giving notice. Notice is effective upon receipt provided that a duplicate copy of the notice is promptly given by first class mail, or the recipient delivers a written confirmation of receipt.

20. No Partnership

This Agreement does not create a partnership relationship. Neither party has authority to enter into contracts on the other's behalf.

21. Applicable Law

This Agreement will be governed by the laws of the State of _____.

[ ] 22. (Optional: Check if applicable.) Assignment and Delegation
Either Contractor or Client may assign its rights or may delegate its duties under this Agreement.

Signatures

Client:

_____ {Name of Client]

By: _____
    Signature

_____ [Typed or Printed Name]

Title: _____

Date: _____

Contractor:

_____ [Name of Contractor]

By: _____
    Signature

_____ [Typed or Printed Name]

Title: _____

Taxpayer ID Number: _____

Date: _____

Independent Contractor Agreement for General Contractor

This Agreement is made between _____ ("Client"), with a principal place of business at _____, and _____ ("Contractor"), with a principal place of business at _____.

1. Services to be Performed

(Check and complete applicable provision.)

[ ] Contractor agrees to perform the following services: _____
_____

OR:

[ ] Contractor agrees to perform the services described in Exhibit A, which is attached to and made part of this Agreement.

2. Payment

(Check and complete applicable provision.)

[ ] In consideration for the services to be performed by Contractor, Client agrees to pay Contractor $.

OR:

[ ] In consideration for the services to be performed by Contractor, Client agrees to pay Contractor at the rate of $ _____ per.

(Optional: Check and complete if applicable.)

[ ] Contractor's total compensation shall not exceed $ _____ without Client's written consent.

3. Terms of Payment

(Check and complete applicable provision.)

[ ] Upon completing Contractor's services under this Agreement, Contractor shall submit an invoice. Client shall pay Contractor within _____ days from the date of Contractor's invoice.

OR:

[ ] Contractor shall be paid $ _____ upon signing this Agreement and the remaining amount due when Contractor completes the services and submits an invoice. Client shall pay Contractor within _____ days from the date of Contractor's invoice.

OR:

[ ] Contractor shall be paid according to the Schedule of Payments set forth in Exhibit attached to and made part of this Agreement.

OR:

[ ] Contractor shall send Client an invoice monthly. Client shall pay Contractor within _____ days from the date of each invoice.

(Optional: Check and complete if applicable.)

[ ] 4. Late Fees

Late payments by Client shall be subject to late penalty fees of _____ % per month from the due date until the amount is paid.

5. Expenses

(Check and complete applicable provision.)

Alternative A
[ ] Contractor shall be responsible for all expenses incurred while performing services under this Agreement.
(Optional: Check if applicable.)
[ ] However, Client shall reimburse Contractor for all reasonable travel and living expenses necessarily incurred by Contractor while away from Contractor's regular place of business to perform services under this Agreement. Contractor shall submit an itemized statement of such expenses. Client shall pay Contractor within 30 days from the date of each statement.
OR:
Alternative B
[ ] Client shall reimburse Contractor for the following expenses that are directly attributable to work performed under this Agreement:
- travel expenses other than normal commuting, including airfares, rental vehicles and highway mileage in company or personal vehicles at __ cents per mile
- telephone, fax, online and telegraph charges
- postage and courier services
- printing and reproduction
- computer services, and
- other expenses resulting from the work performed under this Agreement.

Contractor shall submit an itemized statement of Contractor's expenses. Client shall pay Contractor within 30 days from the date of each statement.
(Optional: Check if applicable.)
[ ] 6. Materials
Contractor will furnish all materials and equipment used to provide the services required by this Agreement.
7. Term of Agreement

This agreement will become effective when signed by both parties and will terminate on the earlier of:
- the date Contractor completes the services required by this Agreement
- _____ [date], or
- the date a party terminates the Agreement as provided below.

8. Terminating the Agreement

(Check and complete applicable provision.)

[ ] With reasonable cause, either party may terminate this Agreement effective immediately by giving written notice of termination for cause. Reasonable cause includes:
- a material violation of this Agreement, or
- nonpayment of Contractor's compensation after 20 days written demand for payment.

Contractor shall be entitled to full payment for services performed prior to the effective date of termination.

OR:

[ ] Either party may terminate this Agreement at any time by giving _____ days written notice of termination. Contractor shall be entitled to full payment for services performed prior to the date of termination.

9. Independent Contractor Status

Contractor is an independent contractor, not Client's employee. Contractor's employees or subcontractors are not Client's employees. Contractor and Client agree to the following rights consistent with an independent contractor relationship.
- Contractor has the right to perform services for others during the term of this Agreement.
- Contractor has the sole right to control and direct the means, manner and method by which the services required by this Agreement will be performed.
- Contractor has the right to hire assistants as subcontractors, or to use employees to provide the services required by this Agreement.

- The Contractor or Contractor's employees or subcontractors shall perform the services required by this Agreement; Client shall not hire, supervise or pay any assistants to help Contractor.
- Neither Contractor nor Contractor's employees or subcontractors shall receive any training from Client in the skills necessary to perform the services required by this Agreement.
- Client shall not require Contractor or Contractor's employees or subcontractors to devote full time to performing the services required by this Agreement.
- Neither Contractor nor Contractor's employees or subcontractors are eligible to participate in any employee pension, health, vacation pay, sick pay or other fringe benefit plan of Client.

10. Local, State and Federal Taxes

Contractor shall pay all income taxes and FICA (Social Security and Medicare taxes) incurred while performing services under this Agreement. Client will not:

- withhold FICA from Contractor's payments or make FICA payments on Contractor's behalf
- make state or federal unemployment compensation contributions on Contractor's behalf, or
- withhold state or federal income tax from Contractor's payments.

The charges included here do not include taxes. If Contractor is required to pay any federal, state or local sales, use, property or value added taxes based on the services provided under this Agreement, the taxes shall be separately billed to Client. Contractor shall not pay any interest or penalties incurred due to late payment or nonpayment of any taxes by Client.

11. Exclusive Agreement

This is the entire Agreement between Contractor and Client.
(Optional: Check if applicable.)
[ ] 12. Modifying the Agreement
This Agreement may be modified only by a writing signed by both parties.

13. Resolving Disputes

(Choose Alternative A, B or C and any desired optional clauses.)

Alternative A

If a dispute arises under this Agreement, any party may take the matter to court.

(Optional: Check if applicable.)

[ ] If any court action is necessary to enforce this Agreement, the prevailing party shall be entitled to reasonable attorney fees, costs and expenses in addition to any other relief to which he or she may be entitled.

Alternative B

If a dispute arises under this Agreement, the parties agree to first try to resolve the dispute with the help of a mutually agreed-upon mediator in _____ [List city or county where mediation will occur]. Any costs and fees other than attorney fees associated with the mediation shall be shared equally by the parties. If the dispute is not resolved within 30 days after it is referred to the mediator, any party may take the matter to court.

(Optional: Check if applicable.)

[ ] If any court action is necessary to enforce this Agreement, the prevailing party shall be entitled to reasonable attorney fees, costs and expenses in addition to any other relief to which he or she may be entitled.

Alternative C

If a dispute arises under this Agreement, the parties agree to first try to resolve the dispute with the help of a mutually agreed-upon mediator in _____ [List city or county where mediation will occur]. Any costs and fees other than attorney fees associated with the mediation shall be shared equally by the parties. If it proves impossible to arrive at a mutually satisfactory solution through mediation, the parties agree to submit the dispute to a mutually agreed-upon arbitrator in _____ [List city or county where arbitration will occur]. Judgment upon the award rendered by the arbitrator may be entered in any court having jurisdiction to do so. Costs of arbitration, including attorney fees, will be allocated by the arbitrator.

(Optional: Check if applicable.)

[ ] 14. Limited Liability

This provision allocates the risks under this Agreement between Contractor and Client. Contractor's pricing reflects the allocation of risk and limitation of liability specified below.

Contractor's total liability to Client under this Agreement for damages, costs and expenses, shall not exceed $ _____ or the compensation received by Contractor under this Agreement, whichever is less. However, contractor shall remain liable for bodily injury or personal property damage resulting from grossly negligent or willful actions of Contractor or Contractor's employees or agents while on Client's premises to the extent such actions or omissions were not caused by Client.

NEITHER PARTY TO THIS AGREEMENT SHALL BE LIABLE FOR THE OTHER'S LOST PROFITS, OR SPECIAL, INCIDENTAL OR CONSEQUENTIAL DAMAGES, WHETHER IN AN ACTION IN CONTRACT OR TORT, EVEN IF THE PARTY HAS BEEN HAS BEEN ADVISED BY THE OTHER PARTY OF THE POSSIBILITY OF SUCH DAMAGES.

15. Notices

All notices and other communications in connection with this Agreement shall be in writing and shall be considered given as follows:

- when delivered personally to the recipient's address as stated on this Agreement;
- three days after being deposited in the United States mail, with postage prepaid to the recipient's address as stated on this Agreement; or
- when sent by fax or telex to the last fax or telex number of the recipient known to the person giving notice; such notice is effective upon receipt provided that a duplicate copy of the notice is promptly given

by first class mail, or the recipient delivers a written confirmation of receipt.

16. No Partnership

This Agreement does not create a partnership relationship. Neither party has authority to enter into contracts on the other's behalf.

17. Applicable Law

This Agreement will be governed by the laws of the State of _____ _____.

18. Assignment

[ ] Either Contractor or Client may assign its rights and may delegate its duties under this Agreement.

OR:

[ ] Contractor may not assign or subcontract any rights or delegate any of its duties under this Agreement without Client's prior written approval.

Signatures

Client:

_____ {Name of Client]

By: _____
    Signature

_____ [Typed or Printed Name]

Title: _____

Date: _____

Contractor:

_____ [Name of Contractor]

By: _____
    Signature

_____ [Typed or Printed Name]

Title: _____

Taxpayer ID Number: _____

Date: _____

Independent Contractor Agreement for Accountant & Bookkeeper

This Agreement is made between _____ ("Client"), with a principal place of business at _____, and _____ ("Contractor"), with a principal place of business at _____.

1. Services to be Performed
(Check and complete applicable provision.)
[ ] Contractor agrees to perform the following services: _____

OR:
[ ] Contractor agrees to perform the services described in Exhibit A, which is attached to and made part of this Agreement.

2. Payment
(Check and complete applicable provision.)
[ ] In consideration for the services to be performed by Contractor, Client agrees to pay Contractor $ _____.

OR:
[ ] In consideration for the services to be performed by Contractor, Client agrees to pay Contractor at the rate of $ _____ [state amount] per hour.

(Optional: Check and complete if applicable.)
[ ] Contractor's total compensation shall not exceed $ _____ without Client's written consent.

3. Terms of Payment
(Check and complete applicable provision.)
[ ] Upon completing Contractor's services under this Agreement, Contractor shall submit an invoice. Client shall pay Contractor within _____ days from the date of Contractor's invoice.

OR:
[ ] Contractor shall be paid $ _____ upon signing this Agreement and the remaining amount due when Contractor completes the services and

submits an invoice. Client shall pay Contractor within _____ days from the date of Contractor's invoice.
OR:
[ ] Contractor shall send Client an invoice monthly. Client shall pay Contractor within _____ days from the date of each invoice.
(Optional: Check and complete if applicable.)
[ ] 4. Late Fees
Late payments by Client shall be subject to late penalty fees of _____ % per month from the due date until the amount is paid.
5. Expenses
Client shall reimburse Contractor for the following expenses that are directly attributable to work performed under this Agreement:
- travel expenses other than normal commuting, including airfares, rental vehicles, and highway mileage in company or personal vehicles at cents per mile
- telephone, fax, online and telegraph charges
- postage and courier services
- printing and reproduction
- computer services, and
- other expenses resulting from the work performed under this Agreement.

Contractor shall submit an itemized statement of Contractor's expenses. Client shall pay Contractor within 30 days from the date of each statement.
6. Materials
Client shall make available to Contractor, at Client's expense, the following materials: _____.
These items will be provided to Contractor by _____.
7. Term of Agreement
This Agreement will become effective when signed by both parties and will end no later than _____.
8. Terminating the Agreement
(Check applicable provision.)

[ ] With reasonable cause, either party may terminate this Agreement effective immediately by giving written notice of cause for termination. Reasonable cause includes:
- a material violation of this Agreement, or
- nonpayment of Contractor's compensation after 20 days written demand for payment.

Contractor shall be entitled to full payment for services performed prior to the effective date of termination.

OR:

[ ] Either party may terminate this Agreement at any time by giving _____ days written notice of termination. Contractor shall be entitled to full payment for services performed prior to the date of termination.

9. Independent Contractor Status

Contractor is an independent contractor, not Client's employee. Contractor's employees or subcontractors are not Client's employees. Contractor and Client agree to the following rights consistent with an independent contractor relationship.
- Contractor has the right to perform services for others during the term of this Agreement.
- Contractor has the sole right to control and direct the means, manner and method by which the services required by this Agreement will be performed.
- Contractor has the right to hire assistants as subcontractors, or to use employees to provide the services required by this Agreement.
- The Contractor or Contractor's employees or subcontractors shall perform the services required by this Agreement; Client shall not hire, supervise or pay any assistants to help Contractor.
- Neither Contractor nor Contractor's employees or subcontractors shall receive any training from Client in the skills necessary to perform the services required by this Agreement.

- Client shall not require Contractor or Contractor's employees or subcontractors to devote full time to performing the services required by this Agreement.
- Neither Contractor nor Contractor's employees or subcontractors are eligible to participate in any employee pension, health, vacation pay, sick pay or other fringe benefit plan of Client.

10. Professional Obligations

Contractor shall perform all services under this Agreement in accordance with generally accepted accounting practices and principles. This Agreement is subject to the laws, rules and regulations governing the accounting profession imposed by government authorities or professional associations of which Contractor is a member.

11. Local, State and Federal Taxes

Contractor shall pay all income taxes and FICA (Social Security and Medicare taxes) incurred while performing services under this Agreement. Client will not:
- withhold FICA from Contractor's payments or make FICA payments on Contractor's behalf
- make state or federal unemployment compensation contributions on Contractor's behalf, or
- withhold state or federal income tax from Contractor's payments.

The charges included here do not include taxes. If Contractor is required to pay any federal, state or local sales, use, property or value added taxes based on the services provided under this Agreement, the taxes shall be separately billed to Client. Contractor shall not pay any interest or penalties incurred due to late payment or nonpayment of any taxes by Client.

12. Exclusive Agreement

This is the entire Agreement between Contractor and Client.
(Optional: Check if applicable.)
[ ] 13. Modifying the Agreement
Client and Contractor recognize that:

- Contractor's original cost and time estimates may be too low due to unforeseen events, or to factors unknown to Contractor when this Agreement was made
- Client may desire a mid-project change in Contractor's services that would add time and cost to the project and possibly inconvenience Contractor, or
- Other provisions of this Agreement may be difficult to carry out due to unforeseen circumstances.

If any intended changes or any other events beyond the parties' control require adjustments to this Agreement, the parties shall make a good faith effort to agree on all necessary particulars. Such agreements shall be put in writing, signed by the parties and added to this Agreement.

14. Resolving Disputes

(Choose Alternative A, B or C and any desired optional clauses.)

      Alternative A

[ ] If a dispute arises under this Agreement, any party may take the matter to court.

(Optional: Check if applicable.)

[ ] If any court action is necessary to enforce this Agreement, the prevailing party shall be entitled to reasonable attorney fees, costs and expenses in addition to any other relief to which he or she may be entitled.

      Alternative B

[ ] If a dispute arises under this Agreement, the parties agree to first try to resolve the dispute with the help of a mutually agreed-upon mediator in _____ [List city or county where mediation will occur]. Any costs and fees other than attorney fees associated with the mediation shall be shared equally by the parties. If the dispute is not resolved within 30 days after it is referred to the mediator, any party may take the matter to court.

(Optional: Check if applicable.)

[ ] If any court action is necessary to enforce this Agreement, the prevailing party shall be entitled to reasonable attorney fees, costs and expenses in addition to any other relief to which he or she may be entitled.

Alternative C

[ ] If a dispute arises under this Agreement, the parties agree to first try to resolve the dispute with the help of a mutually agreed-upon mediator in _____ [List city or county where mediation will occur]. Any costs and fees other than attorney fees associated with the mediation shall be shared equally by the parties. If it proves impossible to arrive at a mutually satisfactory solution through mediation, the parties agree to submit the dispute to a mutually agreed-upon arbitrator in _____ [List city or county where arbitration will occur]. Judgment upon the award rendered by the arbitrator may be entered in any court having jurisdiction to do so. Costs of arbitration, including attorney fees, will be allocated by the arbitrator.

15. Notices

All notices and other communications in connection with this Agreement shall be in writing and shall be considered given as follows:

- when delivered personally to the recipient's address as stated on this Agreement
- three days after being deposited in the United States mail, with postage prepaid to the recipient's address as stated on this Agreement, or
- when sent by fax or telex to the last fax or telex number of the recipient known to the person giving notice; such notice is effective upon receipt provided that a duplicate copy of the notice is promptly given by first class mail, or the recipient delivers a written confirmation of receipt.

16. No Partnership

This Agreement does not create a partnership relationship. Neither party has authority to enter into contracts on the other's behalf.

17. Applicable Law
This Agreement will be governed by the laws of the State of _____.

Signatures
Client:
_____ {Name of Client]
By: _____
   Signature
_____ [Typed or Printed Name]
Title: _____
Date: _____
Contractor:
_____ [Name of Contractor]
By: _____
   Signature
_____ [Typed or Printed Name]
Title: _____
Taxpayer ID Number: _____
Date: _____

Independent Contractor Agreement for Consultant

This Agreement is made between _____ ("Client") with a principal place of business at _____, and _____ ("Consultant"), with a principal place of business at _____.

1. Services to be Performed
(Check and complete applicable provision.)
[ ] Consultant agrees to perform the following services on Client's behalf: _____.

OR:
[ ] Consultant agrees to perform the services described in Exhibit A, which is attached to this Agreement.

2. Payment
(Check and complete applicable provision.)
[ ] In consideration for the services to be performed by Consultant, Client agrees to pay Consultant $ _____.
OR:
[ ] In consideration for the services to be performed by Consultant, Client agrees to pay Consultant at the rate of $ _____ [state amount] per _____.
(Optional: Check and complete if applicable.)
[ ] Consultant's total compensation shall not exceed $ _____ without Client's written consent.

3. Terms of Payment
(Check and complete applicable provision.)
[ ] Upon completing Consultant's services under this Agreement, Consultant shall submit an invoice. Client shall pay Consultant within _____ days from the date of Consultant's invoice.
OR:
[ ] Consultant shall be paid $ _____ upon signing this Agreement and the remaining amount due when Consultant completes the services and submits an invoice. Client shall pay Consultant within _____ days from the date of Consultant's invoice.
OR:
[ ] Consultant shall be paid according to the Schedule of Payments set forth in Exhibit ___ attached to and made part of this Agreement.
OR:
[ ] Consultant shall send Client an invoice monthly. Client shall pay Consultant within _____ days from the date of each invoice.
(Optional: Check and complete if applicable.)
[ ] 4. Late Fees
Late payments by Client shall be subject to late penalty fees of _____ % per month from the due date until the amount is paid.

5. Expenses
(Check and complete applicable provision.)

Alternative A

[ ] Contractor shall be responsible for all expenses incurred while performing services under this Agreement.

(Optional: Check if applicable.)

[ ] However, Client shall reimburse Contractor for all reasonable travel and living expenses necessarily incurred by Contractor while away from Contractor's regular place of business to perform services under this Agreement. Contractor shall submit an itemized statement of such expenses. Client shall pay Contractor within 30 days from the date of each statement.

OR:

Alternative B

[ ] Client shall reimburse Contractor for the following expenses that are directly attributable to work performed under this Agreement:

- travel expenses other than normal commuting, including airfares, rental vehicles and highway mileage in company or personal vehicles at ___ cents per mile
- telephone, fax, online and telegraph charges
- postage and courier services
- printing and reproduction
- computer services, and
- other expenses resulting from the work performed under this Agreement.

Contractor shall submit an itemized statement of Contractor's expenses. Client shall pay Contractor within 30 days from the date of each statement.

(Optional: Check if applicable.)

[ ] 6. Materials

Consultant will furnish all materials, equipment and supplies used to provide the services required by this Agreement.

(Optional: Check if applicable.)

[ ] 7. Intellectual Property Ownership

[ ] Consultant grants to Client a royalty-free nonexclusive license to use anything created or developed by Consultant for Client under this

Agreement (Contract Property). The license shall have a perpetual term and Client may not transfer it. Consultant shall retain all copyrights, patent rights and other intellectual property rights to the Contract Property.

OR:

[ ] Consultant assigns to Client all patent, copyright and trade secret rights in anything created or developed by Consultant for Client under this Agreement. This assignment is conditioned upon full payment of the compensation due Consultant under this Agreement.

Consultant shall help prepare any documents Client considers necessary to secure any copyright, patent or other intellectual property rights at no charge to Client. However, Client shall reimburse Consultant for reasonable out-of-pocket expenses.

(Optional: Check and complete if applicable.)

[ ] 8. Consultant's Reusable Materials

Consultant owns or holds a license to use and sublicense various materials in existence before the start date of this Agreement (Consultant's Materials). Consultant's Materials include, but are not limited to, those items identified in Exhibit _____, attached to and made part of this Agreement. Consultant may, at its option, include Consultant's Materials in the work performed under this Agreement. Consultant retains all right, title and interest, including all copyrights, patent rights and trade secret rights in Consultant's Materials. Consultant grants Client a royalty-free nonexclusive license to use any Consultant's

Materials incorporated into the work performed by Consultant under this Agreement. The license shall have a perpetual term and may not be transferred by Client.

9. Term of Agreement

This agreement will become effective when signed by both parties and will terminate on the earlier of:

- the date Contractor completes the services required by this Agreement

- _____ [date], or
- the date a party terminates the Agreement as provided below.

10. Terminating the Agreement

(Check and complete applicable provision.)

[ ] With reasonable cause, either party may terminate this Agreement effective immediately by giving written notice of cause for termination. Reasonable cause includes:
- a material violation of this Agreement, or
- nonpayment of Consultant's compensation after 20 days written demand for payment.

Consultant shall be entitled to full payment for services performed prior to the effective date of termination.

OR:

[ ] Either party may terminate this Agreement at any time by giving _____ days written notice of termination. Consultant shall be entitled to full payment for services performed prior to the date of termination.

11. Independent Contractor Status

Consultant is an independent contractor, not Client's employee. Consultant's employees or subcontractors are not Client's employees. Consultant and Client agree to the following rights consistent with an independent contractor relationship.
- Consultant has the right to perform services for others during the term of this Agreement.
- Consultant has the sole right to control and direct the means, manner and method by which the services required by this Agreement will be performed.
- Consultant has the right to hire assistants as subcontractors, or to use employees to provide the services required by this Agreement.
- Consultant or Consultant's employees or subcontractors shall perform the services required by this Agreement; Client shall not hire, supervise or pay any assistants to help Consultant.

- Neither Consultant nor Consultant's employees or subcontractors shall receive any training from Client in the skills necessary to perform the services required by this Agreement.
- Client shall not require Consultant or Consultant's employees or subcontractors to devote full time to performing the services required by this Agreement.
- Neither Consultant nor Consultant's employees or subcontractors are eligible to participate in any employee pension, health, vacation pay, sick pay or other fringe benefit plan of Client.

12. Local, State and Federal Taxes

Consultant shall pay all income taxes and FICA (Social Security and Medicare taxes) incurred while performing services under this Agreement. Client will not:
- withhold FICA from Consultant's payments or make FICA payments on Consultant's behalf
- make state or federal unemployment compensation contributions on Consultant's behalf, or
- withhold state or federal income tax from Consultant's payments.

The charges included here do not include taxes. If Consultant is required to pay any federal, state or local sales, use, property or value added taxes based on the services provided under this Agreement, the taxes shall be separately billed to Client. Consultant shall not pay any interest or penalties incurred due to late payment or nonpayment of any taxes by Client.

13. Exclusive Agreement

This is the entire Agreement between Consultant and Client.
(Optional: Check if applicable.)
[ ] 14. Modifying the Agreement

Client and Consultant recognize that:
- Consultant's original cost and time estimates may be too low due to unforeseen events, or to factors unknown to Consultant when this Agreement was made

- Client may desire a mid-project change in Consultant's services that would add time and cost to the project and possibly inconvenience Consultant, or
- Other provisions of this Agreement may be difficult to carry out due to unforeseen circumstances.

If any intended changes or any other events beyond the parties' control require adjustments to this Agreement, the parties shall make a good faith effort to agree on all necessary particulars. Such agreements shall be put in writing, signed by the parties and added to this Agreement.

15. Resolving Disputes

(Choose Alternative A, B or C and any desired optional clauses.)

Alternative A

[ ] If a dispute arises under this Agreement, any party may take the matter to court.

(Optional: Check if applicable.)

[ ] If any court action is necessary to enforce this Agreement, the prevailing party shall be entitled to reasonable attorney fees, costs and expenses in addition to any other relief to which he or she may be entitled.

Alternative B

[ ] If a dispute arises under this Agreement, the parties agree to first try to resolve the dispute with the help of a mutually agreed-upon mediator in _____ [List city or county where mediation will occur]. Any costs and fees other than attorney fees associated with the mediation shall be shared equally by the parties. If the dispute is not resolved within 30 days after it is referred to the mediator, any party may take the matter to court.

(Optional: Check if applicable.)

[ ] If any court action is necessary to enforce this Agreement, the prevailing party shall be entitled to reasonable attorney fees, costs and expenses in addition to any other relief to which he or she may be entitled.

Alternative C

[ ] If a dispute arises under this Agreement, the parties agree to first try to resolve the dispute with the help of a mutually agreed-upon mediator in

_____ [List city or county where mediation will occur]. Any costs and fees other than attorney fees associated with the mediation shall be shared equally by the parties. If it proves impossible to arrive at a mutually satisfactory solution through mediation, the parties agree to submit the dispute to a mutually agreed-upon arbitrator in _____ [List city or county where arbitration will occur]. Judgment upon the award rendered by the arbitrator may be entered in any court having jurisdiction to do so. Costs of arbitration, including attorney fees, will be allocated by the arbitrator.

(Optional: Check if applicable.)

[ ] 16. Limited Liability

This provision allocates the risks under this Agreement between Contractor and Client. Contractor's pricing reflects the allocation of risk and limitation of liability specified below.

Contractor's total liability to Client under this Agreement for damages, costs and expenses, shall not exceed $ _____ or the compensation received by Contractor under this Agreement, whichever is less. However, contractor shall remain liable for bodily injury or personal property damage resulting from grossly negligent or willful actions of Contractor or Contractor's employees or agents while on Client's premises to the extent such actions or omissions were not caused by Client.

NEITHER PARTY TO THIS AGREEMENT SHALL BE LIABLE FOR THE OTHER'S LOST PROFITS, OR SPECIAL, INCIDENTAL OR CONSEQUENTIAL DAMAGES, WHETHER IN AN ACTION IN CONTRACT OR TORT, EVEN IF THE PARTY HAS BEEN HAS BEEN ADVISED BY THE OTHER PARTY OF THE POSSIBILITY OF SUCH DAMAGES.

17. Notices

All notices and other communications in connection with this Agreement shall be in writing and shall be considered given as follows:

- when delivered personally to the recipient's address as stated on this Agreement

- three days after being deposited in the United States mail, with postage prepaid to the recipient's address as stated on this Agreement, or
- when sent by fax or telex to the last fax or telex number of the recipient known to the person giving notice.

Notice is effective upon receipt provided that a duplicate copy of the notice is promptly given by first class mail, or the recipient delivers a written confirmation of receipt.

18. No Partnership

This Agreement does not create a partnership relationship. Neither party has authority to enter into contracts on the other's behalf.

19. Applicable Law

This Agreement will be governed by the laws of the State of _____ _____.

(Optional: Check if applicable.)

[ ] 20. Assignment and Delegation

Either Contractor or Client may assign its rights or may delegate its duties under this Agreement.

Signatures

Client:

_____ {Name of Client]

By: _____
   Signature

_____ [Typed or Printed Name]

Title: _____

Date: _____

Contractor:

_____ [Name of Contractor]

By: _____
   Signature

_____ [Typed or Printed Name]

Title: _____

Taxpayer ID Number: _____
Date: _____

Independent Contractor Agreement for Direct Seller

This Agreement is made between _____ ("Client"), with a principal place of business at _____, and _____ ("Contractor"), with a principal place of business at _____ _____.

1. Services to be Performed

Contractor agrees to sell the following product or merchandise for owner: _____

(Optional: Check if applicable.)
[ ] Contractor shall seek sales of the product in the homes of various individuals.

2. Compensation

In consideration for the services to be performed by Contractor, Client agrees to pay Contractor a commission on completed sales as follows: _____

Contractor acknowledges that no other compensation is payable by Client, and that all of Contractor's compensation will depend on sales made by Contractor. None of Contractor's compensation shall be based on the number of hours worked by Contractor.

(Optional: Check and complete if applicable.)
[ ] 3. Late Fees

Late payments by Client shall be subject to late penalty fees of _____ % per month from the due date until the amount is paid.

4. Expenses

(Check and complete applicable provision.)
[ ] Contractor shall be responsible for all expenses incurred while performing services under this Agreement. This includes license fees, memberships and dues; automobile and other travel expenses; meals and entertainment; insurance premiums; and all salary, expenses and other

compensation paid to employees or contract personnel the Contractor hires to complete the work under this Agreement.
OR:
[ ] Client shall reimburse Contractor for the following expenses that are directly attributable to work performed under this Agreement: _____

_____
Contractor shall submit an itemized statement of Contractor's expenses. Client shall pay Contractor within 30 days after receipt of each statement.
(Optional: Check if applicable.)
[ ] 5. Materials
Contractor will furnish all materials and equipment used to provide the services required by this Agreement.

6. Term of Agreement

This agreement will become effective when signed by both parties and will terminate on the earlier of:
- the date Contractor completes the services required by this Agreement,
- _____ [date], or
- the date a party terminates the Agreement as provided below.

7. Terminating the Agreement

(Check applicable provision.)
[ ] With reasonable cause, either party may terminate this Agreement effective immediately by giving written notice of cause for termination. Reasonable cause includes:
- a material violation of this Agreement, or
- nonpayment of Contractor's compensation after 20 days written demand for payment.

Contractor shall be entitled to full payment of all commissions earned on orders received by Client prior to the effective date of termination.
OR:
[ ] Either party may terminate this Agreement at any time by giving _____ days written notice of termination. Contractor shall be entitled to

full payment of all commissions earned on orders received by Client prior to the effective date of termination.

8. Independent Contractor Status

Contractor is an independent contractor, not Client's employee. Contractor's employees or contract personnel are not Client's employees. Contractor and Client agree to the following rights consistent with an independent contractor relationship.

- Contractor has the right to perform services for others during the term of this Agreement.
- Contractor shall have no obligation to perform any services other than the sale of the product described here.
- Contractor has the sole right to control and direct the means, manner and method by which the services required by this Agreement will be performed. Consistent with this freedom from Client's control, Contractor:
  - does not have to pursue or report on leads furnished by Client
  - is not required to attend sales meetings organized by Client
  - does not have to obtain Client's pre-approval for orders, and
  - shall adopt and carry out its own sales strategy.
- Subject to any restrictions on Contractor's sales territory contained in this Agreement, Contractor has the right to perform the services required by this Agreement at any location or time.
- Contractor has the right to hire assistants as subcontractors, or to use employees to provide the services required by this Agreement, except that Client may supply Contractor with sales forms.
- The Contractor or Contractor's employees or contract personnel shall perform the services required by this Agreement; Client shall not hire, supervise or pay any assistants to help Contractor.
- Neither Contractor nor Contractor's employees or contract personnel shall receive any training from Client in the skills necessary to perform the services required by this Agreement.

- Client shall not require Contractor or Contractor's employees or contract personnel to devote full time to performing the services required by this Agreement.

9. Local, State and Federal Taxes

Contractor shall pay all income taxes and FICA (Social Security and Medicare taxes) incurred while performing services under this Agreement. Client will not:
- withhold FICA from Contractor's payments or make FICA payments on Contractor's behalf
- make state or federal unemployment compensation contributions on Contractor's behalf, or
- withhold state or federal income tax from Contractor's payments.

The charges included here do not include taxes. If Contractor is required to pay any federal, state or local sales, use, property or value added taxes based on the services provided under this Agreement, the taxes shall be separately billed to Client. Contractor shall not pay any interest or penalties incurred due to late payment or nonpayment of any taxes by Client.

10. Exclusive Agreement

This is the entire Agreement between Contractor and Client.
(Optional: Check if applicable.)
[ ] 11. Confidentiality

During the term of this Agreement and for months/years afterward, Contractor will use reasonable care to prevent the unauthorized use or dissemination of Client's confidential information. Reasonable care means at least the same degree of care Contractor uses to protect its own confidential information from unauthorized disclosure.

Confidential information is limited to information clearly marked as confidential, or disclosed orally and summarized and identified as confidential in a writing delivered to Contractor within 15 days of disclosure. Confidential information does not include information that:
- the Contractor knew before Client disclosed it
- is or becomes public knowledge through no fault of Contractor

- Contractor obtains from sources other than Client who owe no duty of confidentiality to Client, or
- Contractor independently develops.

12. Resolving Disputes

(Choose Alternative A, B or C and any desired optional clauses.)

Alternative A

[ ] If a dispute arises under this Agreement, any party may take the matter to court.

(Optional: Check if applicable.)

[ ] If any court action is necessary to enforce this Agreement, the prevailing party shall be entitled to reasonable attorney fees, costs and expenses in addition to any other relief to which he or she may be entitled.

Alternative B

[ ] If a dispute arises under this Agreement, the parties agree to first try to resolve the dispute with the help of a mutually agreed-upon mediator in _____ [List city or county where mediation will occur]. Any costs and fees other than attorney fees associated with the mediation shall be shared equally by the parties. If the dispute is not resolved within 30 days after it is referred to the mediator, any party may take the matter to court.

(Optional: Check if applicable.)

[ ] If any court action is necessary to enforce this Agreement, the prevailing party shall be entitled to reasonable attorney fees, costs and expenses in addition to any other relief to which he or she may be entitled.

Alternative C

[ ] If a dispute arises under this Agreement, the parties agree to first try to resolve the dispute with the help of a mutually agreed-upon mediator in _____ [List city or county where mediation will occur]. Any costs and fees other than attorney fees associated with the mediation shall be shared equally by the parties. If it proves impossible to arrive at a mutually satisfactory solution through mediation, the parties agree to submit the dispute to a mutually agreed-upon arbitrator in _____ [List

city or county where arbitration will occur]. Judgment upon the award rendered by the arbitrator may be entered in any court having jurisdiction to do so. Costs of arbitration, including attorney fees, will be allocated by the arbitrator.

13. Notices

All notices and other communications in connection with this Agreement shall be in writing and shall be considered given as follows:
- when delivered personally to the recipient's address as stated on this Agreement
- three days after being deposited in the United States mail, with postage prepaid to the recipient's address as stated on this Agreement, or
- when sent by fax or telex to the last fax or telex number of the recipient known to the person giving notice. Notice is effective upon receipt provided that a duplicate copy of the notice is promptly given by first class mail, or the recipient delivers a written confirmation of receipt.

14. No Partnership

This Agreement does not create a partnership relationship. Contractor does not have authority to enter into contracts on Client's behalf.

15. Applicable Law

This Agreement will be governed by the laws of the State of _____ _____.

(Optional: Check if applicable.)

[ ] 16. Assignment and Delegation

Either Contractor or Client may assign its rights and may delegate its duties under this Agreement.

Signatures

Client:

_____ {Name of Client]

By: _____
    Signature

_____ [Typed or Printed Name]
Title: _____
Date: _____
Contractor:
_____ [Name of Contractor]
By: _____
    Signature
_____ [Typed or Printed Name]
Title: _____
Taxpayer ID Number: _____
Date: _____

_____ {Name of Client]
By: _____
    Signature
_____ [Typed or Printed Name]
Title: _____
Date: _____
Contractor:
_____ [Name of Contractor]
By: _____
    Signature
_____ [Typed or Printed Name]
Title: _____
Taxpayer ID Number: _____
Date: _____

Independent Contractor Agreement for Work Made for Hire

This Agreement is made between _____ (Client) with a principal place of business at _____ _____ and _____

_____ (Contractor), with a principal place of business at: _____
_____.
This Agreement will become effective on _____, _____ and will end no later than _____, _____.

Services to Be Performed
(Check and complete applicable provision.)
___ Contractor agrees to perform the following services:
_____
_____

OR
___ Contractor agrees to perform the services described in Exhibit A, which is attached to this Agreement.
_____
_____

Payment
(Check and complete applicable provision.)
___ In consideration for the services to be performed by Contractor, Client agrees to pay Contractor $_____ according to the terms set out below.

OR
___ In consideration for the services to be performed by Contractor, Client agrees to pay Contractor at the rate of $_____ per _____ according to the terms of payment set out below.

Additional Option
(Check and complete applicable provision.)
____ Unless otherwise agreed in writing, Client's maximum liability for all services performed during the term of this Agreement shall not exceed $_____.

Terms of Payment

(Check applicable provision.)

___ Upon completing Contractor's services under this Agreement, Contractor shall submit an invoice. Client shall pay Contractor the compensation described within a reasonable time after receiving Contractor's invoice.

OR

___ Contractor shall be paid $_____ upon signing this Agreement and the rest of the sum described above when the Contractor completes services and submits an invoice.

OR

___ Client shall pay Contractor according to the following schedule of payments:

1) $_____ when an invoice is submitted and the following services are complete:

2) $_____ when an invoice is submitted and the following services are complete:

3) $_____ when an invoice is submitted and the following services are complete:

OR

___ Contractor shall submit an invoice to Client on the last day of each month for the work performed during that month. The invoice should include: an invoice number, the dates covered by the invoice, the hours expended and a summary of the work performed. Client shall pay Contractor's fee within a reasonable time after receiving the invoice.

Expenses

Contractor shall be responsible for all expenses incurred while performing services under this Agreement. This includes license fees, memberships and dues; automobile and other travel expenses; meals and entertainment; insurance premiums; and all salary, expenses and other compensation paid to employees or contract personnel the Contractor hires to complete the work under this Agreement.

Independent Contractor Status

Contractor is an independent contractor, not Client's employee. Contractor's employees or contract personnel are not Client's employees. Contractor and Client agree to the following rights consistent with an independent contractor relationship.
* Contractor has the right to perform services for others during the term of this Agreement.
* Contractor has the sole right to control and direct the means, manner and method by which the services required by this Agreement will be performed.
* Contractor has the right to perform the services required by this Agreement at any place, location or time.
* Contractor will furnish all equipment and materials used to provide the services required by this Agreement.
* Contractor has the right to hire assistants as subcontractors, or to use employees to provide the services required by this Agreement.
* The Contractor or Contractor's employees or contract personnel shall perform the services required by this Agreement; Client shall not hire, supervise or pay any assistants to help Contractor.
* Neither Contractor nor Contractor's employees or contract personnel shall receive any training from Client in the skills necessary to perform the services required by this Agreement.
* Client shall not require Contractor or Contractor's employees or contract personnel to devote full time to performing the services required by this Agreement.

Intellectual Property Ownership

To the extent that the work performed by Contractor under this Agreement (Contractor's Work) includes any work of authorship entitled to protection under the copyright laws, the parties agree to the following provisions.
* Contractor's Work has been specially ordered and commissioned by Client as a contribution to a collective work, a supplementary work

or other category of work eligible to be treated as a work made for hire under the United States Copyright Act.

* Contractor's Work shall be deemed a commissioned work and a work made for hire to the greatest extent permitted by law.
* Client shall be the sole author of Contractor's Work and any work embodying the Contractor's Work according to the United States Copyright Act.
* To the extent that Contractor's Work is not properly characterized as a work made for hire, Contractor grants to Client all right, title and interest in Contractor's Work, including all copyright rights, in perpetuity and throughout the world.
* Contractor shall help prepare any papers Client considers necessary to secure any copyrights, patents, trademarks or intellectual property rights at no charge to Client. However, Client shall reimburse Contractor for reasonable out-of-pocket expenses incurred.
* Contractor agrees to require any employees or contract personnel Contractor uses to perform services under this Agreement to assign in writing to Contractor all copyright and other intellectual property rights they may have in their work product. Contractor shall provide Client with a signed copy of each such assignment.

Optional Addition:
(Check if applicable.)

___ Contractor agrees not to use any of the intellectual property mentioned above for the benefit of any other party without Client's prior written permission.

Confidentiality

Contractor will not disclose or use, either during or after the term of this Agreement, any proprietary or confidential information of Client without Client's prior written permission except to the extent necessary to perform services on Client's behalf.

Proprietary or confidential information includes:

- the written, printed, graphic or electronically recorded materials furnished by Client for Contractor to use
- business plans, customer lists, operating procedures, trade secrets, design formulas, know-how and processes, computer programs and inventories, discoveries and improvements of any kind, and
- information belonging to customers and suppliers of Client about whom Contractor gained knowledge as a result of Contractor's services to Client.

Contractor shall not be restricted in using any material which is publicly available, already in Contractor's possession or known to Contractor without restriction, or which is rightfully obtained by Contractor from sources other than Client.

Upon termination of Contractor's services to Client, or at Client's request, Contractor shall deliver to Client all materials in Contractor's possession relating to Client's business.

State and Federal Taxes

Client will not:
- withhold FICA (Social Security and Medicare taxes) from Contractor's payments or make FICA payments on Contractor's behalf
- make state or federal unemployment compensation contributions on Contractor's behalf, or
- withhold state or federal income tax from Contractor's payments.

Contractor shall pay all taxes incurred while performing services under this Agreement—including all applicable income taxes and, if Contractor is not a corporation, self-employment (Social Security) taxes. Upon demand, Contractor shall provide Client with proof that such payments have been made.

Fringe Benefits

Contractor understands that neither Contractor nor Contractor's employees or contract personnel are eligible to participate in any employee pension, health, vacation pay, sick pay or other fringe benefit plan of Client.

Workers' Compensation

Client shall not obtain workers' compensation insurance on behalf of Contractor or Contractor's employees. If Contractor hires employees to perform any work under this Agreement, Contractor will cover them with workers' compensation insurance and provide Client with a certificate of workers' compensation insurance before the employees begin the work.

Optional Language
(Check if applicable.)

____ If not operating as a corporation, Contractor shall obtain workers' compensation insurance coverage for Contractor. Contractor shall provide Client with proof that such coverage has been obtained before starting work.

Unemployment Compensation

Client shall make no state or federal unemployment compensation payments on behalf of Contractor or Contractor's employees or contract personnel. Contractor will not be entitled to these benefits in connection with work performed under this Agreement.

Insurance

Client shall not provide any insurance coverage of any kind for Contractor or Contractor's employees or contract personnel. Contractor agrees to maintain an insurance policy of at least $_____ to cover any negligent acts committed by Contractor or Contractor's employees or agents while performing services under this Agreement.

Contractor shall indemnify and hold Client harmless from any loss or liability arising from performing services under this Agreement.

Terminating the Agreement
(Check applicable provision.)

____ With reasonable cause, either Client or Contractor may terminate this Agreement, effective immediately upon giving written notice. Reasonable cause includes:
- * a material violation of this Agreement, or
- * any act exposing the other party to liability to others for personal injury or property damage.

OR

_____ Either party may terminate this Agreement any time by giving thirty days written notice to the other party of the intent to terminate.

Exclusive Agreement
This is the entire Agreement between Contractor and Client.

Severability
If any part of this Agreement is held unenforceable, the rest of the Agreement will continue in effect.

Applicable Law
This Agreement will be governed by the laws of the state of _____ _____.

Notices
All notices and other communications in connection with this Agreement shall be in writing and shall be considered given as follows:
* when delivered personally to the recipient's address as stated on this Agreement
* three days after being deposited in the United States mail, with postage prepaid to the recipient's address as stated on this Agreement, or
* when sent by fax or telex to the last fax or telex number of the recipient known to the person giving notice. Notice is effective upon receipt provided that a duplicate copy of the notice is promptly given by first class mail, or the recipient delivers a written confirmation of receipt.

No Partnership
This Agreement does not create a partnership relationship. Contractor does not have authority to enter into contracts on Client's behalf.

Resolving Disputes
If a dispute arises under this Agreement, any party may take the matter to court.

Additional Option

If any court action is necessary to enforce this Agreement, the prevailing party shall be entitled to reasonable attorney fees, costs and expenses in addition to any other relief to which he or she may be entitled.

OR

If a dispute arises under this Agreement, the parties agree to first try to resolve the dispute with the help of a mutually agreed-upon mediator in _____. Any costs and fees other than attorney fees associated with the mediation shall be shared equally by the parties.

If the dispute is not resolved within 30 days after it is referred to the mediator, any party may take the matter to court.

Additional Option
If any court action is necessary to enforce this Agreement, the prevailing party shall be entitled to reasonable attorney fees, costs and expenses in addition to any other relief to which he or she may be entitled.

OR

If a dispute arises under this Agreement, the parties agree to first try to resolve the dispute with the help of a mutually agreed-upon mediator in _____. Any costs and fees other than attorney fees associated with the mediation shall be shared equally by the parties.

If it proves impossible to arrive at a mutually satisfactory solution through mediation, the parties agree to submit the dispute to a mutually agreed upon arbitrator in _____. Judgment upon the award rendered by the arbitrator may be entered in any court having jurisdiction to do so. Costs of arbitration, including attorney fees, will be allocated by the arbitrator.

Signatures
Client:
Name of Client: _____
By: _____
         (Signature)
_____
(Typed or Printed Name)
Title: _____
Date: _____
Contractor:
Name of Contractor: _____
By: _____
         (Signature)
_____
(Typed or Printed Name)
Taxpayer ID Number: _____
Date: _____

If Agreement Is Faxed:
Contractor and Client agree that this Agreement will be considered signed when the signature of a party is delivered by facsimile transmission. Signatures transmitted by facsimile shall have the same effect as original signatures.

Contract Amendment Form

This Amendment is made between _____ and _____ _____ to amend the Original Agreement titled _____ _____, signed by them on _____.
The Original Agreement is amended as follows: _____

All provisions of the Original Agreement, except as modified by this Amendment, remain in full force and effect and are reaffirmed. If there is any conflict between this Amendment and any provision of the Original Agreement, the provisions of this Amendment shall control.

Signatures
Client:
_____ [Name of Client]
By: _____
   Signature
_____ [Typed or Printed Name]
Title: _____
Date: _____
Contractor:
_____ [Name of Contractor]
By: _____
   Signature
_____ [Typed or Printed Name]
Title: _____
Taxpayer ID Number: _____
Date: _____

least $_____ to cover any negligent acts committed by Contractor or Contractor's employees or agents while performing services under this Agreement.

Additional Agreement Clauses

Intellectual Property Ownership

Contractor assigns to Client all patent, copyright and trade secret rights in anything created or developed by Contractor for Client under this Agreement. Contractor shall help prepare any documents Client considers necessary to secure any copyright, patent or other intellectual property rights at no charge to Client. However, Client shall reimburse Contractor for reasonable out-of-pocket expenses.

Names of Independent Contractor and Hiring Firm
This Agreement is made between _____ [Your company name] (Client) with a principal place of business at [your business address] and _____ [Contractor 's name] (Contractor), with a principal place of business at _____ [Contractor's address].

Non-Solicitation
For a period of _____ after termination of this Agreement, Contractor agrees not to call on, solicit or take away Client's customers or potential customers of which Contractor became aware as a result of Contractor's services for Client.

Payment
**Alternative A
In consideration for the services to be performed by Contractor, Client agrees to pay Contractor $ _____ [State amount] according to the terms set out below.

**Alternative B
In consideration for the services to be performed by Contractor, Client agrees to pay Contractor at the rate of $ _____ [State amount] per _____ [Hour, day, week or other unit of time] according to the terms of payment set out below.

**Additional Option
Unless otherwise agreed in writing, Client's maximum liability for all services performed during the term of this Agreement shall not exceed $ _____ [State the top limit on what you will pay].

Services to Be Performed

**Alternative A
Contractor agrees to perform the following services: [Briefly describe services you want performed by IC.]

**Alternative B
Contractor agrees to perform the services described in Exhibit A, which is attached to this Agreement.

Unemployment Compensation

Client shall make no state or federal unemployment compensation payments on behalf of Contractor or Contractor's employees or contract personnel. Contractor will not be entitled to these benefits in connection with work performed under this Agreement.

Workers' Compensation

Client shall not obtain workers' compensation insurance on behalf of Contractor or Contractor's employees. If Contractor hires employees to perform any work under this Agreement, Contractor will cover them with workers' compensation insurance and provide Client with a certificate of workers' compensation insurance before the employees begin the work.

**Suggested Optional Language
If not operating as a corporation, Contractor shall obtain workers' compensation insurance coverage for Contractor. Contractor shall provide Client with proof that such coverage has been obtained before starting work.

Work at Your Premises

Because of the nature of the services to be provided by Contractor, Client agrees to furnish space on its premises for Contractor while performing these services.

Terminating the Agreement

**Alternative A
With reasonable cause, either Client or Contractor may terminate this Agreement, effective immediately upon giving written notice. Reasonable cause includes:
* a material violation of this Agreement, or
* any act exposing the other party to liability to others for personal injury or property damage.

**Alternative B
Either party may terminate this Agreement any time by giving _____ [State term of notice] written notice to the other party of the intent to terminate.

State and Federal Taxes
Client will not:
* withhold FICA (Social Security and Medicare taxes) from Contractor's payments or make FICA payments on Contractor's behalf
* make state or federal unemployment compensation contributions on Contractor's behalf, or
* withhold state or federal income tax from Contractor's payments.

Contractor shall pay all taxes incurred while performing services under this Agreement—including all applicable income taxes and, if Contractor is not a corporation, self-employment (Social Security) taxes. Upon demand, Contractor shall provide Client with proof that such payments have been made.

Severability
If any part of this Agreement is held unenforceable, the rest of the Agreement will continue in effect.

Resolving Disputes
If a dispute arises under this Agreement, the parties agree to first try to resolve the dispute with the help of a mutually agreed-upon mediator. If it proves impossible to arrive at a mutually satisfactory solution through mediation, the parties agree to submit their dispute to binding arbitration under the rules of the American Arbitration Association.

Notices
All notices and other communications in connection with this Agreement shall be in writing and shall be considered given as follows:
* when delivered personally to the recipient's address as stated on this Agreement
* three days after being deposited in the United States mail, with postage prepaid to the recipient's address as stated on this Agreement, or
* when sent by fax or telex to the last fax or telex number of the recipient known to the person giving notice. Notice is effective upon receipt provided that a duplicate copy of the notice is promptly given by first class mail, or the recipient delivers a written confirmation of receipt.

No Partnership
This Agreement does not create a partnership relationship. Contractor does not have authority to enter into contracts on Client's behalf.

Modifying the Agreement
This Agreement may be amended only by a writing signed by both Client and Contractor.
Independent Contractor Status

Miscellaneous

Contractor is an independent contractor, not Client's employee. Contractor's employees or contract personnel are not Client's employees. Contractor and Client agree to the following rights consistent with an independent contractor relationship.

* Contractor has the right to perform services for others during the term of this Agreement.
* Contractor has the sole right to control and direct the means, manner and method by which the services required by this Agreement will be performed.
* Contractor has the right to perform the services required by this Agreement at any place, location or time.
* Contractor will furnish all equipment and materials used to provide the services required by this Agreement.
* Contractor has the right to hire assistants as subcontractors, or to use employees to provide the services required by this Agreement.
* The Contractor or Contractor's employees or contract personnel shall perform the services required by this Agreement; Client shall not hire, supervise or pay any assistants to help Contractor.
* Neither Contractor nor Contractor's employees or contract personnel shall receive any training from Client in the skills necessary to perform the services required by this Agreement.
* Client shall not require Contractor or Contractor's employees or contract personnel to devote full time to performing the services required by this Agreement.

OPTIONAL:
* Contractor acknowledges that Contractor has been classified as an independent contractor because such classification is a longstanding practice of a significant segment of Client's trade or industry.

Insurance
Client shall not provide any insurance coverage of any kind for Contractor or Contractor's employees or contract personnel. Contractor agrees to maintain an insurance policy of at least $ _____ [State amount] to cover any negligent acts committed by Contractor or Contractor's employees or agents while performing services under this Agreement.

Indemnity
Contractor shall indemnify and hold Client harmless from any loss or liability arising from performing services under this Agreement.

Fringe Benefits
Contractor understands that neither Contractor nor Contractor's employees or contract personnel are eligible to participate in any employee pension, health, vacation pay, sick pay or other fringe benefit plan of Client.

Exclusive Agreement
This is the entire Agreement between Contractor and Client.

Business Permits, Certificates and Licenses
Contractor has complied with all federal, state and local laws requiring business permits, certificates and licenses required to carry out the services to be performed under this Agreement.

Assignment

**Alternative A
Either Contractor or Client may assign, delegate or subcontract any rights or obligations under this Agreement.

**Alternative B
Contractor may not assign, delegate or subcontract any rights or obligations under this Agreement without Client's prior written approval.

CHAPTER 20

THE IRS IS ON OUR SIDE

This Training Manual is not provided in its entirety. The entire paper can be found on the IRS website.

DEPARTMENT OF THE TREASURY • INTERNAL REVENUE SERVICE INDEPENDENT CONTRACTOR OR EMPLOYEE? TRAINING MATERIALS THIS MATERIAL WAS DESIGNED SPECIFICALLY FOR TRAINING PURPOSES ONLY. UNDER NO CIRCUMSTANCES SHOULD THE CONTENTS BE USED OR CITED AS AUTHORITY FOR SETTING OR SUSTAINING A TECHNICAL POSITION.
Training 3320-102(10-96)
TPDS 84238I
October 30, 1996
FOREWORD
Examiners and other Internal Revenue Service (IRS) representatives are sometimes faced with the difficult task of making a determination of the

classification of workers who provide products and services for others. The status of a worker as either an independent contractor or employee must be determined accurately to ensure that workers and businesses can anticipate and meet their tax responsibilities timely and accurately. Businesses decide whether to hire employees or independent contractors depending on individual needs, customer expectations, and worker availability. Either worker classification—independent contractor or employee—can be a valid and appropriate business choice.

The majority of classifications of workers are not challenged by the IRS. When they are, there is usually agreement between the IRS and the business after the facts and circumstances are jointly reviewed. Nonetheless, when the IRS determines there may be a need for reclassification to accurately reflect the relationship of the worker and the business, the legal standard for distinguishing between independent contractor and employee can be difficult to apply. Also, the importance of indicators that might help in applying the legal standard can change and should be reviewed from time to time.

This training addresses the application of section 530 of the Revenue Act of 1978. Section 530 can in certain circumstances relieve businesses of employment tax liability resulting from worker classification. This training provides you with the tools to make legally correct determinations of worker classifications. It also discusses facts that may indicate the existence of an independent contractor or an employer-employee relationship and guides you in determining which facts are most relevant under the common law standard. It emphasizes that relevant facts may change over time because business relationships and the work environment change over time. In addition, it addresses how to determine whether workers are statutory employees.

IRS policy requires its employees to exercise strict impartiality in the conduct of their duties. Thus, you must approach the issue of worker classification in a fair and impartial manner and actively consider section 530 relief at the beginning of an examination. This includes furnishing taxpayers with a summary of section 530 at the beginning of an examination. Additionally, you may need to assist taxpayers in identifying facts which establish either worker classification.

In this course This course has been developed to provide Employment Tax Specialists and Revenue Officer Examiners with the tools to make worker classifications. The lessons will cover a review of the issues, law, and examination techniques for making a correct determination; as well as a review of Section 530 relief.

INDEPENDENT CONTRACTOR OR EMPLOYEE: DOES SECTION 530 APPLY?

INTRODUCTION

530 relief Section 530 provides businesses with relief from federal employment tax obligations if certain requirements are met. It terminates the business's, not the worker's, employment tax liability under Internal Revenue Code (IRC) Subtitle C (Federal Insurance Contributions Act (FICA) and Federal Unemployment Tax Act (FUTA) taxes, federal income tax withholding, and Railroad Retirement Tax Act taxes) and any interest or penalties attributable to the liability for employment taxes (Rev. Proc. 85-18, 1985-1 C.B. 518).

Section 530(e)(3) of the Revenue Act of 1978, as amended by the Small Business Job Protection Act of 1996, clarifies that the first step in any case involving whether the business has the employment tax obligations of an employer with respect to workers is determining whether the business meets the requirements of section 530. If so, the business will not have an employment tax liability with respect to the workers at issue. Objectives At the end of this lesson, you will be able to:

1. Explain the two consistency requirements that must be met for a business to obtain relief under section 530.
2. Explain the reasonable basis test that must be met for a business to obtain relief under section 530.
3. Explain the three safe havens under the reasonable basis test.
4. Determine whether relief is applicable in a particular situation.

INTRODUCTION
Overview of requirements

The business must meet the following consistency and reasonable basis requirements before the relief provisions of section 530 apply:

Consistency Test

The business must meet both aspects of the consistency test by:
- filing all required Forms 1099 (reporting consistency)
- treating all workers in similar positions the same (substantive consistency)

Reasonable Basis Test

The business must reasonably rely on one of the following:
- prior audit safe haven
- judicial precedent safe haven
- industry practice safe haven
- other reasonable basis

Meeting the consistency and reasonable basis tests will give the business relief from employment taxes with respect to the workers whose status is in question.

INTRODUCTION
Historical background

Section 530 of the Revenue Act of 1978, as amended, is not part of the Internal Revenue Code (IRC). However, some publishers include its text after IRC section 3401(a). It was originally intended as an "interim" relief measure, but was extended indefinitely by the Tax Equity and Fiscal Responsibility Act of 1982.

Section 530 was amended by section 1706 of the Tax Reform Act of 1986 (1986-3, C.B. (Vol.1) 698). Section 530(d) denies relief for certain technically skilled workers who provide services under a three party situation. It will be discussed in detail later in this lesson.

Section 530(e) was added by section 1122 of the Small Business Job Protection Act of 1996 (H.R. 3448). Section 530(e), which is generally effective after December 31, 1996, contains a number of provisions that affect conditions under which a business will be eligible for section 530 relief. It is discussed throughout this lesson.

INTRODUCTION

Service must consider section 530

It is not necessary for the business to claim section 530 relief for it to be applicable. In order to correctly determine tax liability, as required by the IRS mission, you must explore the applicability of section 530 even if the business does not raise the issue. In addition, a plain language summary of section 530 must be provided to the taxpayer at the beginning of an examination of worker classification

Time to claim section 530 relief

The section 530 analysis is, itself, fact intensive. You will identify the possible application of section 530 relief before beginning the development of the worker classification issue. The relief is available, however, throughout the examination or administrative (including appeals) process, as well as, any subsequent judicial proceeding.

Section 530 limits guidance

When Congress enacted section 530, the IRS was barred from issuing any regulations or revenue rulings pertaining to worker classification. As a result, the IRS cannot issue new revenue rulings or even modify existing revenue rulings to reflect new developments. At the same time, courts have been able to modify their applications of the common law standard in response to factual developments. As a result, courts may now look at the employee versus independent contractor issue somewhat differently—possibly making outstanding IRS revenue rulings outdated and in conflict with judicial decisions. Section 530 imposes no prohibition on private letter rulings or technical advice memoranda. Also there is no prohibition on published guidance dealing with section 530 itself.

INTRODUCTION

Section 530 considered first

Section 530 is a relief provision that should be considered as the first step in any case involving worker classification.

Change from prior policy
Considering section 530 first is a change from prior policy and results from the Small Business Job Protection Act of 1996. New section 530(e)(3) specifies that a worker does not have to be an employee of the business in order for relief to apply. Additionally, the business need not concede or agree to the determination that the workers are employees in order for section 530 relief to be available.

Other tax consequences for workers
A business may be entitled to relief under section 530 but workers may find, through a determination letter or some other means, that they have been misclassified and are employees. However, section 530 relief does not extend to the worker. It does not convert a worker from the status of employee to the status of independent contractor. As noted above, misclassified employees are liable for the employee share of FICA rather than for tax under the Self Employment Tax Contributions Act (SECA). Workers may have filed and paid their own employment tax. If the worker paid SECA, the worker may file a claim for refund for the difference between SECA tax and the employee share of FICA. *See*, Rev. Proc. 85-18, section 3.08; Treas. Reg. section 31.3102-1(c). There are other tax consequences for the worker as well. Workers as employees generally cannot deduct unreimbursed business expenses above the line on Schedule C, but must deduct them, if at all, as miscellaneous itemized deductions on Schedule A, Form 1040, subject to the two-percent limitation of IRC section 67. This sometimes results in liability for the alternative minimum tax. Further, the worker as an employee cannot adopt or maintain a self-employed retirement plan. Finally, certain benefits provided by the business to a worker as an employee may be excludable from income by the employee due to specific IRC exclusions provided only to employees (*e.g.*, employer provided accident and health insurance).

CONSISTENCY TEST: REPORTING CONSISTENCY
Information Returns:Filing information returns

The first requirement a business must meet to obtain relief under section 530 is timely filing of all required Forms 1099 with respect to the worker for the period, on a basis consistent with the business's treatment of the worker as not being an employee. This provision applies only "for the period." Rev. Proc. 85-18, section 3.03(B). That is, if a business in a subsequent year files all required returns on a basis consistent with the treatment of the worker as not being an employee, then the business may qualify for section 530 relief for the subsequent period. If a business is not "required to file," relief will not be denied on the basis that the return was not filed.

CONSISTENCY TEST: REPORTING CONSISTENCY
Information Returns:
Rev. Rul. 81-224 Rev. Rul. 81-224, 1981-2 C.B. 197, addresses specific questions about timely filing of Forms 1099. It provides that:
- businesses that do not file timely Forms 1099 consistent with their treatment of the worker as an independent contractor, may not obtain relief under the provisions of section 530 for that worker in that year
- businesses that mistakenly, in good faith, file the wrong type of Form 1099 do not lose section 530 eligibility

Best source: IRS records
The best source for determining whether Forms 1099 were filed timely is internal IRS records. Service Centers maintain information on the Payer Master File which records the taxpayer's history of filing information returns. These transcripts can be requested internally. Recall that Form 1099, reporting payments of $600 or more, must generally be filed by the last day of February following the close of the year in which the payment for the services was made. However, businesses may apply for extensions of time to file information returns. Relevant cases *General Investment Corp. v. United States*, 823 F. 2d 337 (9th Cir. 1987) The business was not entitled to section 530 relief for the year it failed to file information returns; *Claire W. Murphy v. United States*, 93-2 USTC par. 50,610 (W.D.

WI 1993)—The business was not entitled to protection under section 530 where the business did not provide the required information returns.

CONSISTENCY TEST: SUBSTANTIVE CONSISTENCY

Substantive Consistency required

You will recall from reading section 530 that its provisions do not apply if the business or a predecessor treated the worker, or any worker holding a substantially similar position, as an employee at any time after December 31, 1977. In other words, treatment of the class of workers must be consistent with the business's belief that they were independent contractors.

Substantially similar position

A substantially similar position exists if the job functions, duties, and responsibilities are substantially similar and the control and supervision of those duties and responsibilities are substantially similar. In addition, section 530(e)(6), added by the Small Business Job Protection Act, states that the determination of whether workers hold substantially similar positions requires consideration of the relationship between the taxpayers and those individuals. This includes, but is not limited to, the degree of supervision and control. This statutory change appears to be designed to enable differences in managerial responsibilities and differences in reporting requirements to be taken into account, along with differences in job duties. Presumably, the contractual relationship and the provision of employee benefits are also entitled to some weight.

The determination of what is substantially similar work rests on analysis of the facts. The day-to-day services that workers perform and the method by which they perform those services are relevant in determining whether workers treated as independent contractors hold substantially similar positions to workers treated as employees. Comparison of job functions is an important fact. Workers with significantly different, though overlapping, job functions are not substantially similar.

CONSISTENCY TEST: SUBSTANTIVE CONSISTENCY

Defining treatment

Rev. Proc. 85-18 provides examples of treatment consistent or inconsistent with payments to an independent contractor:
1. The withholding of federal income tax or FICA tax from a worker's wages is treatment of the worker as an employee, whether or not the tax is paid to the Government.
2. Filing a Form 940, 941, 942, 943, or W-2 with respect to a worker, whether or not tax was withheld from the worker, is treatment of the worker as an employee for that period. NOTE: Beginning in 1995, household employers report wages paid to household employees on their individual income tax returns using Schedule H rather than Form 942.
3. The filing of a delinquent or amended employment tax return for a particular tax period is not treatment of the worker as an employee if the filing was a result of IRS compliance procedures. However, filing the returns for periods after the period under audit is "treatment" of the workers as employees for those later periods, regardless of the time at which the return was filed.
4. Neither the use of an IRC section 6020(b) return prepared by the IRS nor the signing of Form 2504 (Agreement to Assessment and Collection of Additional Tax and Acceptance of Overassessment) constitutes treatment.

Demonstrating treatment important—relevant rulings & cases
Both revenue rulings and cases illustrate the importance of demonstrating treatment of workers in periods prior to those under consideration.
- Rev. Rul. 83-16, 1983-1 C.B. 235—Section 530 relief was unavailable to three doctors who had been treated as employees of a medical corporation in 1979 and 1980, but were not treated as employees in 1981 after the doctors created individual trusts to which the corporation made payments for the doctors' services.
- Rev. Rul. 84-161, 1984-2 C.B. 202—A trucking company that had treated its drivers as employees from 1970-1978 began treating them as independent contractors in 1979; section 530 relief was

unavailable because the trucking company had treated them as employees for "any period beginning after 12-31-77."
- *Institute for Resource Management, Inc. v. United States*, 90-2 USTC par. 50,586 (Cl. Ct. 1990)—No safe haven was available for employment tax treatment of any worker who was treated as an independent contractor if the business treated any worker holding a substantially similar position as an employee for employment tax purposes.
- *In re Critical Care Support Services, Inc.*, 138 B.R. 378 (Bankr. E.D.N.Y. 1992)—Section 530 relief was not available because the business, through its predecessor, treated the nurses as employees, the business did not timely file appropriate tax forms, and the business had no reasonable basis for not treating its nurses as employees.

Treatment for state purposes

Only federal tax treatment as an employee is relevant. Thus, if a business treats workers as employees for state unemployment or state withholding tax purposes, that is not treatment for purposes of section 530. However, if the business uses a federal form, such as Form W-2, to report state tax withholding, the filing of the federal form is treatment for purposes of section 530.

Treatment by predecessor

Section 530 specifically states that the treatment by predecessor entities will be taken into account when evaluating substantive consistency. This ensures that the substantive consistency rule is not avoided by the formation of new entities. *See* Rev. Proc. 85-18.

Changing treatment of workers

If the business begins to treat misclassified workers as employees, relief is available under section 530 for the years it treated them as independent contractors, provided it meets both consistency requirements (reporting and substantive consistency) and reasonable basis for the years prior to the change in treatment. *See* Rev. Proc. 85-18, section 3.04. The Small Business Job Protection Act added this rule as section 530 (e)(5).

Dual status Some workers perform services in two capacities. For example, a business's bookkeeper might be separately engaged to design and print an advertising brochure. The fact that the bookkeeper is treated as an employee with respect to the bookkeeping services does not preclude application of section 530 if it is determined that the bookkeeper is an employee, and not an independent contractor, with respect to the design and printing services.

Cases about "substantially similar"

Several cases have discussed the meaning of "substantially similar". Caution should be exercised in using these "substantially similar" cases due to the later enactment of section 530 (e)(6).

- *Lowen Corporation v. United States*, 785 F.Supp. 913 (D. Kan. 1992)—The court granted summary judgment for the Government on the issue of whether the business was entitled to section 530 relief because the business had treated workers holding substantially similar positions as employees. On the issue of worker status, the court (*Lowen v. United States*, 72 AFTR 2d par. 6,350 (D. Kan. 1993)) found that all but 15 of 113 salespersons were independent contractors.
- *REAG, Inc. v. United States*, 801 F. Supp. 494 (W.D. Okla. 1992)— Differing treatment of owner/appraisers and non-owner/appraisers was not inconsistent treatment since the owners had managerial control and performed substantial duties.
- *World Mart, Inc. v. United States*, 93-1 USTC par. 50,304 (D. Ariz. 1992)—No inconsistent treatment was found where probationary telemarketers were treated as independent contractors on the basis that the probationary workers did not hold the "same position" as the regular telemarketers. *Compare In re Compass Marine Corporation*, 146 B.R.138 (Bankr. E.D. Pa. 1992)—Court states that a strong argument could be made that the business failed the consistency requirement of section 530(a)(3) where workers were

treated as independent contractors for a probationary period and then reclassified as employees.

REASONABLE BASIS TEST

Moving to the next step

Once you have determined that the business has met the consistency test, you will address the reasonable basis test.

Reasonable basis test

The business must reasonably rely on one of the following ways to meet the reasonable basis test, as listed in Rev. Proc. 85-18:

REASONABLE BASIS TEST EXPLANATION

Judicial Precedent Safe Haven

Reasonable reliance on judicial precedent; published rulings; a technical advice memorandum, private letter ruling, or determination letter pertaining to the business.

Past Audit Safe Haven Reasonable reliance on a past IRS audit of the business for employment tax purposes, if the audit began after December 31, 1996, and entailed consideration of, but no assessment attributable to the business's employment tax treatment of workers holding positions substantially similar to the position held by the worker whose status is at issue. (NOTE: A business may continue to rely on any audit that began before January 1, 1997, even though the audit was not related to employment tax matters.)

Industry Practice Safe Haven

Reasonable reliance on a long-standing recognized practice of a significant segment of the industry in which the business is engaged. The practice need not be uniform throughout an entire industry.

Other Reasonable Basis

A business which fails to meet any of the three safe havens may nevertheless be entitled to relief, if the business can demonstrate, in some other manner, any reasonable basis for not treating the worker as an employee.

Liberal construction

The Conference Agreement on section 530 of the Revenue Act of 1978 explains Congress' intent that the reasonable basis requirement be construed liberally. Extract H.R. Rep. No. 1748, 95th Cong. 2nd Sess. 4 (1978), 1978-3 C.B. (Vol. 1) 629, 633.

Generally, the bill grants relief if a taxpayer had any reasonable basis for treating workers as other than employees. The committee intends that this reasonable basis requirement be *construed liberally* in favor of taxpayers. (Emphasis added).

The Congressional direction to liberally construe section 530 means that facts which indicate that the conditions of section 530 have been satisfied by a particular business are to be viewed liberally in favor of the business. Liberal construction does not mean that the conditions for obtaining section 530 relief should be discounted or ignored. Failures to satisfy one or more of the conditions for eligibility for section 530 relief are not cured by the requirement of liberal construction of the reasonable basis requirement.

The burden of proof

In the Small Business Job Protection Act, Congress indicated that the business's burden of proof differs from that in ordinary tax cases. As is generally true in tax matters, the business has the initial burden of proof in demonstrating that it is entitled to relief under section 530. See, *Boles Trucking, Inc. v. United States*, 1996 77 F.3rd 236 (8th Cir. 1996).

When burden of proof shifts

However, section (e)(4) shifts the burden of proof to the IRS if two requirements are satisfied:
- The taxpayer establishes a prima facie case that it was reasonable not to treat an individual as an employee.
- The taxpayer cooperates fully with reasonable requests from the examiner.

Which burden of proof shifts

Section 530(e)(3)(4) is designed to codify the holding in *McClellan v. United States*, 900 F.Supp. 101 (E.D. Mich. 1995). In *McClellan*, the court held that if the taxpayer came forward with an explanation and enough evidence to establish prima facie grounds for a finding of reasonableness, then the burden shifted to the IRS to verify or refute the taxpayer's explanation. The shift applies to the reporting consistency requirement (section 530(a)(1)(B); the substantive consistency requirement (section 530(e)(3)); and the three safe havens (judicial precedent, prior audit and industry practice) contained in section 530(a)(2). The shift does not apply in determining whether the taxpayer had any other reasonable basis for treating the worker as an independent contractor.

Prima facie case "Prima facie" means "at first sight" or "on the face of it." A prima facie case means that the taxpayer has presented evidence that will allow the taxpayer to prevail unless the government presents other evidence that contradicts and overcomes the taxpayer's evidence.

Reasonable requests for information

The legislative history of section 530 (e)(4) indicates that the burden of proof shifts only if the taxpayer cooperates fully with all reasonable requests for information relevant to treatment of the worker as an independent contractor. This includes reasonable requests for information relative to filing of returns, treatment of other workers, prior audits, precedent relied upon, and industry practice. However, requests are not reasonable if compliance would be "impracticable given the particular circumstances and relative costs involved." In addition, requests are not reasonable if they relate to a basis other than the one on which the taxpayer relied for establishing its reasonable basis.

Examiners should work with the business to determine what information is needed to conclude whether the business has met the requirements described above. Examiners must exercise caution to ensure requested information is both relevant and reasonable.

Reasonable reliance on safe haven required

Remember that if the business establishes the existence of a safe haven, the business must show reliance on the safe haven. Section 530 requires that the reliance must be reasonable. You should explore with the business why it treated the workers as independent contractors. The business's stated reasons should be set forth in your workpapers. This is important if the case is unagreed, as it provides invaluable information to the appeals officer or attorney. However, the business's stated reasons should also be recorded in agreed cases, as the taxpayer may later file a claim for refund.

REASONABLE BASIS TEST—PRIOR AUDIT

Prior audit We will discuss the second reasonable basis safe haven first because section 530 relief is most easily established by reliance on a prior audit. A business is treated as having reasonable basis if it relied on a prior audit.

Pre-997 audits

For examinations that began before January 1, 1997, the prior IRS audit does not have to have been an audit for employment tax purposes as long as the audit entailed no assessment attributable to the business's treatment, for employment tax purposes, of workers holding positions substantially similar to the position held by the workers whose treatment is at issue. The business need only show that, at the time of the earlier examination, it was treating the same type of workers—as those at issue in the present audit—as independent contractors, and that the treatment went unchallenged or was sustained by the IRS.

Post 1996 audits Section 530(e)(2)(A) limits the prior audit safe haven to audits that included an examination for employment tax purposes of the status of the class of workers at issue or of a substantially similar class of workers. This restriction only applies, however, to audits that begin after December 31,1996. Taxpayers may continue to rely on any audit that began before January 1, 1997, even though the audit was not related to employment tax matters.

Assessment offset by claims

A business does not meet the prior audit test if, in the conduct of a prior examination, an assessment attributable to the business's treatment of the worker(s) was offset by other claims asserted by the business.

Change in work relationship

The prior audit safe haven does not apply if the relationship between the business and the workers is substantially different from that which existed at the time of the audit.

Related entities

The prior audit safe haven is limited to past audits conducted on the business itself. Therefore, a business is not entitled to relief based upon a prior audit of any of its workers. Nor would a subsidiary corporation usually be entitled to relief based upon a prior audit of its separately filing parent corporation. Even if a consolidated return was filed in the year the parent was audited, the subsidiary would only be entitled to relief if the subsidiary was examined in connection with the parent.

If a corporation which was previously audited begins conducting a new line of business, that corporation is not entitled to relief based upon the audit of the corporation's original line of business. However, if there has only been a change of form and the successor entity is in the same line of business, the corporation may nevertheless be entitled to section 530 relief, if the corporation can demonstrate in some other manner, any reasonable basis for not treating the worker as an employee.

Examination of records

A business will be able to claim that it was subject to a prior audit if the IRS previously inspected the business's books and records. Mere inquiries or correspondence from a Service Center will not constitute an audit. If, for example, a correspondence contact was made to verify a discrepancy disclosed by an information matching program, such as Information Returns Processing, self-employment tax, and similar Service Center programs, such contacts do not constitute a prior audit. They are referred to as adjustments. However, if correspondence contacts entailed the examination or inspection of the business's records to determine the accuracy of deductions claimed on a return, such contacts do constitute an audit for purposes of section 530.

Items that are not audits

Even prior to the Small Business Job Protection Act, no prior audit safe haven was created in the following instances:
- an application for status determination, such as an application for recognition for exemption from federal income tax as an exempt organization or an application for a determination letter for an employee benefit plan made on Forms 5300 or 5301
- an examination of an employee benefit plan or consideration of Form 5500 (Annual Return/Report of Employee Benefit Plan) (the plan is generally not the business that engages the workers in question)—(However, an audit that began prior to January 1, 1997, of the business's pension plan that leads to an examination of the business's books and records, such as payroll records, to determine whether coverage requirements have been met may create a safe haven for the business.)
- compliance checks, which ask if a business has filed all required returns, if conducted properly—(However, compliance checks would create a prior audit safe haven, if the IRS asked about the reason for worker classification or examined books and records other than those IRS forms that are required to be filed or maintained.)

Audits by other agencies

Audits conducted by agencies other than the IRS will not qualify a business for relief based upon the prior audit safe haven.

Establishing the fact of prior audit

For examinations that began before January 1, 1997, the business can establish a prima facie case that a prior audit was, in fact, conducted by furnishing a copy of correspondence connected with an IRS audit. If the business states that an audit was conducted in a particular year, and the IRS can verify by existing records that an audit was conducted, the business will be deemed to have met its burden of establishing a prima facie case of the existence of a prior audit. The business also has to show reliance on the prior audit. To show reliance, the business need only show that the same class of workers currently under consideration was treated as independent contractors during the period covered by the prior examination. Of course, the prior audit can only be relied upon for periods after the audit took place. To establish reliance on examinations that began after December 31, 1996, the business must also show that the prior examination included consideration of whether the individual involved (or any individual holding a position substantially similar to the position held by the individual involved) should be treated as an employee of the taxpayer.

REASONABLE BASIS TEST—JUDICIAL PRECEDENT

Judicial precedent

Another safe haven provided by section 530 is judicial precedent. To obtain relief under this section, the business must demonstrate reasonable reliance on a judicial precedent, a published ruling, technical advice relating to that business, or a letter ruling to that business.

Reasonable reliance –judicial precedent

The business must make a prima facie case showing that it reasonably relied upon a particular judicial precedent or published ruling. Because the business must show reasonable reliance, the facts in the case relied upon must be similar to the business's situation. The facts need not be identical and the precedent relied upon need not deal with exactly the same industry as the business's. In addition, the judicial precedent or published ruling relied upon must have been in existence at the time the business began treating workers as independent contractors. As long as these requirements are met, one case is sufficient to establish a precedent that creates a safe haven. This is true even if case law can be found to support either side of the independent contractor/employee issue.

Qualifying TAMS and PLRs

A technical advice memorandum (TAM) or a private letter ruling (PLR) addressing the employer-employee relationship can be used by the business to which it was issued for purposes of the judicial precedent safe haven. If a private letter ruling is issued to a member of a group of related corporations, the business may rely upon the ruling only if it is specifically addressed to that business entity. Note that every corporation included in a related group is considered a separate business entity.

A private letter ruling issued to a business may not be relied upon by its successor. However if there has merely been a change in form, the business may have some "other reasonable basis" on which it could rely. Even a private letter ruling or determination letter issued to the business itself cannot be relied upon if the facts were materially misstated or omitted. Further, if there has been a substantial change in the facts since the ruling or determination was obtained, the precedent does not apply.

Non-qualifying precedents

Section 530 gives businesses relief from federal employment tax obligations. Only federal court decisions and revenue rulings interpreting the IRC are relevant. Businesses are not entitled to the judicial precedent safe haven based upon a state court decision. The term "published rulings" refers to revenue rulings which are intended for general use by all businesses. Neither rulings by state administrative agencies, including agencies which regulate employment, nor rulings from federal agencies other than the IRS can be used to support a judicial precedent safe haven. Under some circumstances, however, state court decisions and state and federal agency rulings may be the basis for findings that the business reasonably relied on some other reasonable basis.

REASONABLE BASIS TEST—INDUSTRY PRACTICE

Industry practice

The safe haven most commonly argued, and the one which causes the most controversy between businesses and the Government, is industry practice. Section 530 states that the business can claim reasonable basis if it can show reasonable reliance on a long-standing recognized practice of a significant segment of the industry in which the business is engaged. It makes sense to begin by defining "industry" since this establishes the group of businesses to be analyzed.

Industry defined

The classic case on the definition of industry is *General Investment Corp. v. United States, supra.* In this case, the Court held that for purposes of the industry practice safe haven, the business's industry consisted of small mining businesses located in the business's county, rather than all mining businesses throughout the country.

Geographic area

An industry generally consists of businesses located in the same geographic or metropolitan area which compete for the same customers. For example, the landscaping industry will generally consist of businesses within a single metropolitan area. However, if the area includes only one or a few businesses in the same industry, the geographic area may be extended to include contiguous areas in which there are other businesses competing for the same customers. If businesses compete in regional or national markets, the geographic area may include the competitors in that region or throughout the United States. For example, the commercial film production industry competes in a national market.

Long-standing

Whether a practice is long-standing depends on facts and circumstances. However, as confirmed by section 530(c)(2)(C), a practice that has existed for 10 years or more should always be treated as long-standing. The business may use the industry practice safe haven even if it began to provide a product or service after 1978. Similarly, a taxpayer may use the industry practice safe haven even if the industry came into existence after 1978. The legislative history clarifies that the 10 year rule is a safe haven. However, a shorter period may be long-standing, depending on the facts and circumstances.

Of course, the business could not have relied on industry practice unless the industry practice was to treat workers as independent contractors prior to the time the business joined the industry. Moreover, if the industry's practice changed by the time the business joined the industry, the business cannot rely on the former practice. Exploring when industry practice began may be necessary in order to determine whether the practice was long-standing.

Significant segment

How prevalent must the practice be to constitute a significant segment and/or recognized practice? Until the Small Business Job Protection Act amended section 530, neither the statute nor the legislative history provided any additional guidance on the appropriate standard for "significant." The determination was made on the basis of facts and circumstances, and it was an issue that often presented difficult analytical issues.

Prior to the Small Business Job Protection Act, courts had indicated that the term "significant segment" did not necessarily require that the practice be followed by a majority of the industry. *See, In re: Joey L. Bentley*, 94-1 USTC par. 50,140 (Bankr. E.D. Tenn. 1994) *aff'd* 94-2 USTC par 50,560 (The court rejected a majority standard as contradicting the plain language of the statute). Section 530 (e)(2)(B) provides that 25 percent of the taxpayer's industry (determined without taking the taxpayer into account) is deemed to constitute a significant segment of the industry. The legislative history notes that a lower percentage may be a significant segment, depending on the facts and circumstances.

Reasonable showing

Section 530(e)(2)(B) requires a "reasonable showing" of industry practice by the taxpayer. Although this language is not explained in the legislative history, it would appear to conform to the burden of proof change discussed above.

Establishing industry practice

Independent contractor treatment often flows from the business's general knowledge of competition in the industry or from communications with competitors or business advisers knowledgeable about the industry. Seldom will the business have performed a formal survey of industry practice at the time treatment of workers as independent contractors began. The fact that a formal survey was not conducted when independent contractor treatment began is relevant to, but is not conclusive of, whether the business relied on industry practice.

Do not automatically reject as irrelevant or immaterial a survey performed at or near the time of the audit. Such a survey can be relevant in establishing a business's prima facie case. The fact that a current survey confirms longstanding industry practice can buttress other evidence that the business relied on industry practice during the relevant period. Discuss with the business, before it begins any survey, the desired sample size, method of selecting the sample, and questions to be asked. The survey should be verifiable or, if anonymity for the businesses contacted is sought, should be conducted by an independent third party.

If the business presents material concerning industry practice that you consider inadequate, do not simply reject that material. Instead, you will need to develop evidence showing why the business's demonstration of industry practice is incorrect or insufficient.

Reasonable reliance

In addition to showing the industry practice at the time it began treating workers as independent contractors, the business must show that its reliance on the industry practice was reasonable. Reasonable reliance contains two concepts that are simple to state but are harder to apply—reasonableness and reliance. The first question to ask is whether the business claiming the industry practice safe haven actually relied on industry practice.

Reliance

At a minimum, reliance requires knowledge. If you don't know something you cannot possibly rely on it. A claim of reliance on industry practice necessarily requires that the business knew of the industry practice at the time when independent contractor treatment began. Thus, the date on which the business's independent contractor treatment began must be determined. The long-standing industry practice must have existed at that time in order to be relied upon. Some evidence of the year of the business's treatment of workers is found by the business's first filing of Forms 1099 for those workers. Evidence of when an industry practice began and of the business's knowledge of that practice is harder to locate and substantiate.

Establishing reliance

Whether the business relied on industry practice can be established by several types of evidence. Examine business records, such as corporate minutes or unanimous consents in lieu of directors' meetings, to determine whether any written record exists that shows the reason for treatment of workers as independent contractors. Interview the workers themselves to determine what reasons were given to them by the business when establishing their status as independent contractors.

Interviews for reliance

Interviewing key workers in the business is also important. In some cases, the business may disclose, or other objective evidence may show, that some reason other than industry practice drove its decision to treat its workers as independent contractors. *See*, for example, Rev. Rul. 82-116, 1982-1 C.B.152, in which the business treated workers as independent contractors because as illegal aliens they failed to obtain social security numbers, not because there was a bona fide dispute about their status as employees. When an industry practice began is not material in this case, because it is clear that an industry practice was not relied upon as the basis for treating the workers as independent contractors.

Establishing that reliance was reasonable

The reliance required to satisfy the industry practice safe haven must be reasonable. Defining "reasonable" is a difficult task, but you might ask yourself: Would a reasonably prudent business under similar circumstances have relied upon such evidence of industry practice to treat workers as independent contractors? The extent of the business's knowledge of industry practice, whether obtained through personal experience, a survey, or through an advisor is relevant in this regard. The reasonableness or unreasonableness of the reliance may turn on the source of the information from which the business derived knowledge of the industry practice. The business's mistaken, but good faith belief concerning industry practice does not qualify it for relief under this safe haven. However, you should be aware that in light of *Diaz v. United States*, 90-1 USTC par. 50,209, a business's good faith misperception of the status of the workers may constitute reasonable cause for waiver of penalties associated with employment tax deficiencies.

OTHER REASONABLE BASIS

Other reasonable basis

A business that fails to meet any of these three safe havens may still be entitled to relief if it can demonstrate that it relied on some other reasonable basis for not treating a worker as an employee. The legislative history indicates that "reasonable basis" should be construed liberally in favor of the taxpayer. H.R. Rep. No. 1748. Remember, the burden of proof does not shift to the IRS here. However, if the business presents an argument that you consider inadequate, you will still need to develop evidence showing why the business's demonstration of other reasonable basis is incorrect or insufficient.

Advice of accountant or attorney

Reliance on the advice of an attorney or accountant may constitute a reasonable basis. The court cases tend to require the business to present (1) evidence of the educational and experiential qualifications of the attorney or accountant, and (2) evidence that the attorney or accountant issued the advice after reviewing relevant facts furnished by the business. *See, In re McAtee*, 90-1 USTC par. 50,242 (N.D. Iowa 1990) *vacating In re McAtee*, 89-2 USTC par. 9,625 (Bankr. N.D. Iowa 1989); *Overeen*, 91-2 USTC par. 50,459 (W.D. Okla. 1991); and *Smokey Mountain Secrets, Inc. v. United States*, 76 AFTR 2d par. 95-5509 (1995).

The business need not independently investigate the credentials of the attorney or accountant to determine whether such advisor has any specialized experience in the employment tax area. However, the business should establish at a minimum, that it reasonably believed the attorney or accountant to be familiar with business tax issues and that the advice was based on sufficient relevant facts furnished by the business to the adviser.

If other evidence shows that the adviser clearly was not qualified, the mere holding of a law or accounting license would not make the business's reliance on the advice reasonable. For example, reliance on the advice of a patent attorney would not be reasonable nor would reliance on the advice of a professional who does not explore the relevant facts. Of course, advice could not have been relied upon unless it had been furnished when treatment of workers as independent contractors began. *See, In re Compass Marine Corporation,* 146 B.R. 138 (Bankr. E.D. Pa 1992) (advice issued three years after the treatment does not support the treatment).

State and non-tax federal law and determinations

Prior state administrative action (*e.g.,* workers' compensation decisions) and other federal determinations (*e.g.,* determinations under the Federal Labor Standards Act (Wage and Hour Division)) may or may not constitute a reasonable basis. This will depend on whether they use the same common law rules that apply for federal employment tax purposes. If the state or federal agency uses the same common law standard and interprets it similarly, however its determination should constitute a reasonable basis. If the state or federal agency uses a different statutory standard or interprets the common law standard differently, its determinations should not constitute a reasonable basis.

- *Queensgate Dental Family Practice, Inc., v. United States,* 91-2 USTC No. 50,536 (M.D. Pa. 1991)—The business treated licensed dentists as independent contractors based on the conclusion by the State Dental Board that state law prohibited a licensed dentist from being an employee of an unlicensed business corporation. The court found this to be "reasonable basis" for section 530 relief.
- *But see, Spicer Accounting, Inc. v. United States,* 918 F. 2d 90 (9th Cir. 1990)—A state's determination that a worker was an independent contractor for state employment tax purposes does not preclude the federal government from challenging the worker's status for federal employment tax purposes if the federal government was not a party, not in privity with the state.

Common law rules
A business that makes a reasonable effort to establish independent contractor treatment for its workers under the common law but falls just short of satisfying the common law standard, may present a valid section 530 safe haven under "other reasonable basis." A reasonable, albeit erroneous, interpretation of the common law rules was found to be sufficient for section 530 relief in *Critical Care Registered Nursing, Inc., supra*, and in *American Institute of Family Relations v. United States*, 79-1 USTC par. 9,364 (C.D.Cal. 1979). A non-acquiescence issued in *Critical Care Registered Nursing, Inc., supra*, (Action on Decision, CC-1194-05, August 8, 1994) does not address this issue.

Prior audit of predecessor
Although a prior audit of the business's predecessor does not satisfy the requirements of the prior audit safe haven, the business may qualify for relief if there has merely been a change in the form of the business. In addition, the successor must be in the same line of business.

PLR/TAM to predecessor
Although a private letter ruling or technical advice memorandum issued to the business's predecessor does not satisfy the requirements of the judicial precedent safe haven, the business may qualify for relief if there has merely been a change in the form of the business. In addition, the successor must be in the same line of business.

Good faith
While a number of types of evidence may support a showing of other reasonable basis, more than a mere good faith belief is required. *See, In re McAtee, supra*. In *In re Compass Marine, supra*, the court cited Senate Report No. 1263, 95th Cong. 2d Sess., at 210 (1978), in dicta, as support for the concept that the business has a "reasonable basis" for section 530 relief if it acted in "good faith." However, the Senate report described actions by a business (such as negligence, intentional disregard of rules and regulations, or fraud) that would not be considered good faith treatment for section 530 relief. It did not cite "good faith" as an affirmative

standard sufficient, by itself, to provide section 530 relief. Thus, although the actions described in the Senate report are sufficient to prevent section 530 relief, their absence is not enough to establish section 530 relief.

Penalties Good faith, although not a sufficient basis for section 530 relief, may be a basis for not asserting penalties. *See, Diaz v. United States, supra.*

Other situations

Lack of worker social security numbers is not a reasonable basis for not treating workers as employees. *See,* Rev. Rul. 82-116—Section 530 relief unavailable to employer who failed to treat illegal aliens as employees because they had no social security numbers. Relief is not available solely because the business treats the workers as independent contractors for competitive cost reasons. Demand by a worker not to have amounts withheld from wages does not constitute some other reasonable basis that entitles the business to relief. *See, Audie D. Moore, Individually and d/b/a A. Moore Distributing v. United States,* 92-2 USTC par. 50,401 (W.D. Mich. 1992)—Workers' agreement to treatment as independent contractors does not constitute a reasonable basis.

WORKERS COVERED BY SECTION 530

Who is covered If a business meets the requirements of section 530 with respect to a group of workers, it is generally not necessary to determine whether the workers are independent contractors or employees. However, it is important to understand the categories of workers to which section 530 can apply, and the category to which it does not apply. The legislative history indicates that section 530 only applies to common law employees. H.R. Rep. No. 95-1748, 95th Cong., 2nd Sess. 4 (1978), 1978-3 C.B. (Vol 1) 629,632. However, section 3.09 of Rev. Proc. 85-18 provides that section 530 applies to ALL employees under section IRC 3121(d).

Officers: IRC section 3121(d)(1)

Officers are generally employees under the IRC. However, as explained in Lesson 3, an officer of a corporation who does not perform any services or performs only minor services and who neither receives nor is entitled to receive directly or indirectly any remuneration is considered not to be an employee. A director, as such, is not an employee. In these two circumstances, the individuals are independent contractors, and section 530 relief would be not applicable . Treas. Reg. section 31.3121(d)-1(b) (FICA); Treas. Reg. section 31.3306(i)-1(e) (FUTA); Treas. Reg. section 31.3401(c)-1(f) (federal income tax withholding).

Rev. Rul. 82-83, 1982-1 C.B. 151

considered whether a corporation could claim section 530 relief with respect to officers' salaries that had been characterized as "draws." The ruling concluded that because there was no reasonable basis for not treating the officers as employees, relief was not available.

Common-law employees:

IRC section 3121(d)(2)

Any worker who is an employee under the common law standard (described in detail in Lesson 2) would be an employee for purposes of section 530.

Statutory employees: IRC

Section 3121(d)(3) IRC section 3121(D)(3) identifies four categories of statutory employees. They are discussed in detail in Lesson 3. Statutory employees include:
- agent-drivers or commission drivers
- full-time life insurance salespersons
- home workers
- traveling or city salespersons.

Statutory employees are employees for purposes of section 530.

Limited applicability to state and local workers covered under 218 Agreement: IRC

Section 3121(d)(4)

Workers covered under a Section 218 Agreement are employees for purposes of FICA without application of the common law rules (IRC section 3121(d)(4)). This classification is not made under rules found in the IRC or the regulations thereunder. The classification is made by the Social Security Act. *See* Lesson 3. For these workers, section 530 relief for FICA taxes is inappropriate, and, therefore, unavailable, because coverage under the Section 218 Agreement is dispositive of the worker's FICA tax status. For federal income tax withholding purposes, the status of workers covered under a Section 218 Agreement is not, however, determined by the Section 218 Agreement but under the common law standard. Section 530 relief is available, retroactively, for federal income tax liability, if the requirements of section 530 are met. The state or local government would be required to withhold federal income tax prospectively. This is because the substantive consistency requirement will fail to be met once the government begins using Form W-2 to report FICA taxes.

Applies to state and local employees not covered under 218 agreement

The common law rules are used to determine the status of a state or local government worker who is not covered under a Section 218 agreement. Relief under section 530 is available for these workers, if the requirements for section 530 relief are satisfied.

WORKERS NOT COVERED BY SECTION 530

Section 530(d) Section 1706 of the Tax Reform Act of 1986 (1986-3, Vol. 1, C.B. 698) (TRA '86), amended section 530 of the Revenue Act of 1978 by adding subsection (d) to that section. Section 530(d) provides that relief under section 530(a) is not available in the case of a worker who, pursuant to an arrangement between the business and a client, provides services for that client as any of the following:

- engineer
- designer
- drafter
- computer programmer
- systems analyst
- other similarly skilled worker engaged in a similar line of work

Applies to three party situations

Note that section 1706 of TRA '86 applies only to the business in a three party situation, namely, the business providing workers to a client. Furthermore, the fact that the worker is incorporated is immaterial. The intent of Congress was to classify, under the common law rules, workers retained by businesses to provide technical services, without regard to section 530 of the Revenue Act of 1978. Section 1706 does not change anyone from independent contractor to employee. The examiner must still look at the common law rules. Section 1706 applies to remuneration paid and services rendered after December 31, 1986.

Prohibition against regulations and rulings lifted

Section 1706 of TRA '86 also lifted the prohibition included in section 530 against the issuance of regulations or rulings concerning employment tax status with respect to workers to whom the amendment applies. In response, the IRS issued Rev. Rul. 87-41,

EFFECT OF SECTION 530 RELIEF ON EMPLOYEE

Status of employee not changed by section 530

As noted previously, section 530 relief does not convert a worker from the status of employee to the status of independent contractor. If it has been determined that worker is an employee, the worker remains an employee for income tax purposes, such as deductions for business expenses and participation in retirement plans.

Liable for employee share of FICA

As previously stated, if the business's liability is terminated by section 530(a)(1), the worker remains liable for employee FICA tax with respect to all wages received. Rev. Proc. 85-18, section 3.08; Treas. Reg. Section 31.3102(c). *See also*, Rev. Rul. 86-111, 1986-2 C.B. 176—The worker remains fully liable for the unwithheld employee FICA tax after the business's liability has been determined under IRC section 3509. The employee's share of FICA tax is reported on Form 4137 by substituting the word "wages" for the word "tips."

SUMMARY

Review of lesson The following summarizes what we have covered in this lesson:

1. Section 530 must be considered as the first step in any worker classification case.

2. Section 530 is a relief provision that has significant impact on the administration of the employment tax laws.
3. Section 530 has been modified, amplified, and defined since 1978 through legislation, IRS revenue rulings, revenue procedures, and court cases. The basic provisions are intact but many interpretation issues remain unresolved.
4. Section 530 provides businesses with relief from federal employment tax obligations if certain requirements are met.
5. The business must meet two consistency requirements before the relief provisions of section 530 apply. For any period after December 31, 1978, the relief applies only if:
    - All Forms 1099 required to be filed by the business with respect to the worker(s), for the period, are timely filed and are filed on a basis consistent with the business's treatment of the worker as an independent contractor; and
    - The treatment of the worker as an independent contractor is consistent with the treatment by the business (predecessor) of all workers holding substantially similar positions for any period beginning after December 31, 1977.
6. In addition to the consistency requirements, the business must have relied on some reasonable basis, including the safe havens of a prior audit, a judicial precedent, or an industry practice.
7. The reasonable basis requirement, including the three safe havens, are to be liberally construed.
8. For examinations beginning before January 1, 1997, a prior audit will provide a safe haven if it is an examination of books and records by the IRS of the same entity, which is still in the same line of business and whose workers are performing substantially the same work. Examinations beginning after December 31, 1996, must have addressed the issue of the status of the class of workers at issue or of a substantially similar class of workers for employment tax purposes.

9. A judicial precedent will provide a safe haven only if the business's case is similar to the precedent. Federal employment tax cases and published rulings qualify. Technical advice memoranda or private letter rulings qualify for the business which requested them. State court decisions and rulings of agencies other than IRS do not qualify.
10. To claim a safe haven under industry practice, the business must show that it is following a long-standing recognized practice of a significant segment of its industry. Industry is the group of businesses that provide the same product or service and compete for the same customers.
11. A business that fails to meet any of the safe havens may be entitled to relief if it can be demonstrated that it relied on some other reasonable basis for not treating the worker as an employee. Text of Section 530, Including Amendments

I. SECTION 530. CONTROVERSIES INVOLVING WHETHER INDIVIDUALS ARE EMPLOYEES FOR PURPOSES OF THE EMPLOYMENT TAXES.

(a) TERMINATION OF CERTAIN EMPLOYMENT TAX LIABILITY.—

(1) In General.—If—

(A) for purposes of employment taxes, the taxpayer did not treat an individual as an employee for any period, and

(B) in the case of periods after December 31, 1978, all Federal tax returns (including information returns) required to be filed by the taxpayer with respect to such individual for such period are filed on a basis consistent with the taxpayer's treatment of such individual as not being an employee, then, for purposes of applying such taxes for such period with respect to the taxpayer, the individual shall be deemed not to be an employee unless the taxpayer had no reasonable basis for not treating such individual as an employee.

(2) STATUTORY STANDARDS PROVIDING ONE METHOD OF SATISFYING THE REQUIREMENTS OF PARAGRAPH (1).—For

purposes of paragraph (1), a taxpayer shall in any case be treated as having a reasonable basis for not treating an individual as an employee for a period if the taxpayer's treatment of such individual for such period was in reasonable reliance on any of the following:

(A) judicial precedent, published rulings, technical advice with respect to the taxpayer, or a letter ruling to the taxpayer;

(B) a past IRS audit of the taxpayer in which there was no assessment attributable to the treatment (for employment tax purposes) of the individuals holding positions substantially similar to the position held by this individual; or

(C) long-standing recognized practice of a significant segment of the industry in which such individual was engaged.

(3) CONSISTENCY REQUIRED IN THE CASE OF PRIOR TAX TREATMENT.—

Paragraph (1) shall not apply with respect to the treatment of any individual for employment tax purposes for any period ending after December 31, 1978, if the taxpayer (or a predecessor) has treated any individual holding a substantially similar position as an employee for purposes of the employment taxes for any period beginning after December 31, 1977.

(4) REFUND OR CREDIT OF OVERPAYMENT.—If refund or credit of any overpayment of an employment tax resulting from the application of paragraph (1) is not barred on the date of the enactment of the Act by any law or rule of law, the period for filing a claim for refund or credit of such overpayment (to the extent attributable to the application of paragraph (1)) shall not expire before the date 1 year after the date of the enactment of this Act.

(b) PROHIBITION AGAINST REGULATIONS AND RULINGS ON EMPLOYMENT

STATUS.—No regulation or Revenue Ruling shall be published on or after the date of the enactment of this Act and before the effective date of any law hereafter enacted clarifying the employment status of individuals for purposes of the employment tax by the Department of the Treasury (including the IRS) with respect to the employment status of any individual for purposes of the employment taxes.

(c) DEFINITIONS.—For purposes of this section—

(1) EMPLOYMENT TAX.—the term "employment tax" means any tax imposed by subtitle C of the IRC of 1954.

(2) EMPLOYMENT STATUS.—The term "employment status" means the status of an individual, under the usual common law rules applicable in determining the employer-employee relationship, as an employee or as an independent contractor (or other individual who is not an employee).

(d) EXCEPTION.—This section shall not apply in the case of an individual who, pursuant to an arrangement between the taxpayer and another person, provides services for such other person as an engineer, designer, drafter, computer programmer, systems analyst, or other similarly skilled worker engaged in a similar line of work.

Small Business Job Protection Act

SEC. 1122. SPECIAL RULES RELATING TO DETERMINATION WHETHER INDIVIDUALS ARE EMPLOYEES FOR PURPOSES OF EMPLOYMENT TAXES.

(a) In General.—section 530 of the Revenue Act of 1978 is amended by adding at the end the following new subsection:

"(e) Special Rules for Application of section.—

"(1) Notice of availability of section.—An officer or employee of the Internal Revenue Service shall, before or at the commencement of any audit inquiry relating to the employment status of one or more individuals who perform services for the taxpayer, provide the taxpayer with a written notice of the provisions of this section.

"(2) Rules relating to statutory standards.—For purposes of subsection (a)(2)—"(A) a taxpayer may not rely on an audit commenced after December 31, 1996, for purposes of subparagraph (B) thereof unless such audit included an examination for employment tax purposes of whether the individual involved (or any individual holding a position substantially similar to the position held by the individual involved) should be treated as an employee of the taxpayer,

"(B) in no event shall the significant segment requirement of subparagraph (C) thereof be construed to require a reasonable showing of the practice of more than 25 percent of the industry (determined by not taking into account the taxpayer), and

"(C) in applying the long-standing recognized practice requirement of subparagraph(C) thereof—

"(i) such requirement shall not be construed as requiring the practice to have continued for more than 10 years, and

"(ii) a practice shall not fail to be treated as long-standing merely because such practice began after 1978.

"(3) Availability of safe harbors.—Nothing in this section shall be construed to provide that subsection (a) only applies where the individual involved is otherwise an employee of the taxpayer.

"(4) Burden of proof.—

"(A) In general.—If—

"(i) a taxpayer establishes a prima facie case that it was reasonable not to treat an individual as an employee for purposes of this section, and

"(ii) the taxpayer has fully cooperated with reasonable requests from the Secretary of the Treasury or his delegate, then the burden of proof with respect to such treatment shall be on the Secretary.

"(B) Exception for other reasonable basis.—In the case of any issue involving whether the taxpayer had a reasonable basis not to treat an individual as an employee for purposes of this section, subparagraph (A) shall only apply for purposes of determining whether the taxpayer meets the requirements of subparagraph (A), (B), or

(C) of subsection (a)(2).

"(5) Preservation of prior period safe harbor.—If—

"(A) an individual would (but for the treatment referred to in subparagraph (B)) be deemed not to be an employee of the taxpayer under subsection (a) for any prior period, and

"(B) such individual is treated by the taxpayer as an employee for employment tax purposes for any subsequent period, then, for purposes of applying such taxes for such prior period with respect to the taxpayer, the individual shall be deemed not to be an employee.

"(6) Substantially similar position.—For purposes of this section, the determination as to whether an individual holds a position substantially similar to a position held by another individual shall include consideration of the relationship between the taxpayer and such individuals."

(b) Effective Dates.—

(1) In general.—The amendment made by this section shall apply to periods after December 31, 1996.

(2) Notice by Internal Revenue Service.—section 530(e)(1) of the Revenue Act of 1978 (as added by subsection (a)) shall apply to audits which commence after December 31, 1996.

(3) Burden of proof.—

(A) In general.—section 530(e)(4) of the Revenue Act of 1978 (as added by subsection (a)) shall apply to disputes involving periods after December 31, 1996.

(B) No inference.—Nothing in the amendments made by this section shall be construed to infer the proper treatment of the burden of proof with respect to disputes involving periods before January 1, 1997.

DEPARTMENT OF THE TREASURY • INTERNAL REVENUE SERVICE INDEPENDENT CONTRACTOR OR EMPLOYEE? SECTION 530 RELIEF REQUIREMENTS SECTION 530 PROVIDES BUSINESSES WITH RELIEF FROM FEDERAL EMPLOYMENT TAX OBLIGATIONS IF CERTAIN REQUIREMENTS ARE MET.

Department of the Treasury
Internal Revenue Service
Publication 1976 (9-96)
Catalog Number 22927M

Your business has been selected for an employment tax examination to determine whether you correctly treated certain workers as independent contractors. However, you will not owe employment taxes for these workers, if you meet the relief requirements described below. If you do not meet these relief requirements, the IRS will need to determine whether the workers are independent contractors or employees and whether you owe employment taxes for those workers.

Section 530 Relief

Requirements:

To receive relief, you must meet all three of the following requirements:

I. Reasonable Basis

First, you had a reasonable basis for not treating the workers as employees. To establish that you had a reasonable basis for not treating the workers as employees, you can show that:

You reasonably relied on a court case about Federal taxes or a ruling issued to you by the IRS; or

Your business was audited by the IRS at a time when you treated similar workers as independent contractors and the IRS did not reclassify those workers as employees; or

You treated the workers as independent contractors because you knew that was how a significant segment of your industry treated similar workers; or

You relied on some other reasonable basis. For example, you relied on the advice of a business lawyer or accountant who knew the facts about your business.

If you did not have reasonable basis for treating the workers as independent contractors, you do not meet the relief requirements.

II. Substantive Consistency

In addition, you (and any predecessor business) must have treated the workers, and any similar workers, as independent contractors. If you treated similar workers as employees, this relief provision is not available.

III. Reporting Consistency

Finally, you must have filed Form 1099-MISC for each worker, unless the worker earned less than $600. Relief is not available for any year you did not file the required Forms1099-MISC. If you filed the required Forms

1099-MISC for some workers, but not for others, relief is not available for the workers for whom you did not file Forms 1099-MISC.

The IRS examiner will answer any questions you may have about your eligibility for this relief.

INDEPENDENT CONTRACTOR OR EMPLOYEE: THE COMMON LAW STANDARD

INTRODUCTION

A worker is an employee if…

IRC section 3121(d) contains four categories of employee for purposes of the FICA. A worker is an employee if he or she is one of the following:
- a common law employee
- a corporate officer
- an employee as defined by statute, commonly referred to as a "statutory employee"
- an employee covered by an agreement under Section 218 of the Social Security Act

The common law test applies also for purposes of the FUTA, federal income tax withholding, and the Railroad Retirement Tax Act.

A worker is not an employee if…

By statute, workers in three occupations are not treated as employees (commonly referred to as "statutory non-employees") for purposes of FICA, FUTA, or federal income tax withholding, provided they meet specific qualifications.

INTRODUCTION

In this lesson…In this lesson, we will review three categories of evidence. Each category contains several related facts which illustrate the right to direct and control—or its absence. All facts must be weighed to determine whether a worker is a common law employee.

Objectives At the end of this lesson, you will be able to:
1. Identify the three categories of evidence.
2. Identify facts that demonstrate the right to direct and control—or its absence—within the categories of evidence.

3. Properly determine if a worker is an independent contractor or a common law employee for federal employment tax purposes.

COMMON LAW EMPLOYEE: CONTROL STANDARD

Common law standard

In determining a worker's status, the primary inquiry is whether the worker is an independent contractor or an employee under the common law standard.

The common law, a major part of the justice system in the United States, flows chiefly from court decisions. Under the common law, the treatment of a worker as an independent contractor or an employee originates from the legal definitions developed in the law of agency—whether one party, the principal, is legally responsible for the acts or omissions of another party, the agent—and depends on the principal's right to direct and control the agent.

The right to direct and control

Following the common law standard, the employment tax regulations provide that an employer-employee relationship exists when the business for which the services are performed has the right to direct and control the worker who performs the services. This control refers not only to the result to be accomplished by the work, but also the means and details by which that result is accomplished. In other words, a worker is subject to the will and control of the business not only as to what work shall be done but also how it shall be done. It is not necessary that the business actually direct or control the manner in which the services are performed; it is sufficient if the business has the right to do so.

Control test

To determine whether the control test is satisfied in a particular case, the facts and circumstances must be examined. Questions about the relationship between the worker and the business are asked to ascertain the degree of control.

Over the years, the IRS and Social Security Administration compiled a list of 20 factors used in court decisions to determine worker status. These 20 factors were eventually published in Rev. Rul. 87-41 and are sometimes called the Twenty Factor Test. Remember, however, that this Twenty Factor Test is an analytical tool and not the legal test used for determining worker status. The legal test is whether there is a right to direct and control the means and details of the work.

COMMON LAW EMPLOYEE: CONTROL STANDARD

Control facts change over time

The twenty common law factors listed in Rev. Rul. 87-41 are not the only ones that may be important. Every piece of information that helps determine the extent to which the business retains the right to control the worker is important. In addition, the relative importance and weight of the twenty common law factors can vary significantly.

Bear in mind also that information important in helping determine worker status may change over time because business relationships change over time. As a result, some of the twenty common law factors listed in Rev. Rul. 87-41 are no longer as relevant as they once were.

See, Weber v. Commissioner, 103 T.C. 378 (1994), *aff'd per curiam* 60 F.3rd 1104 (4th Cir. 1995); *Professional and Executive Leasing, Inc. v. Commissioner*, 862 F.2d 751 (9th Cir. 1988); *Avis Rent-A-Car System, Inc. v. United States*, 503 F.2d 423 (2d Cir. 1974); *Simpson v. Commissioner*, 64 T.C. 974 (1975); *Kenney v. Commissioner*, T.C. Memo 1995-431.

Understand Business operations

In determining worker classification, try to gain an understanding of the way a business operates. Focus on what the business does and how the job gets done. It is also important to understand the relationship between the business and its clients or customers.

COMMON LAW EMPLOYEE: CONTROL STANDARD

Examining the relationship

A correct determination can only be made by examining the relationship of the worker and the business. It is important to remember that the result can be either that the worker is an independent contractor or an employee. Normally, our audit process is designed to select returns with a high probability of error for audit. However, a case which results in a "no change" does not indicate there is a problem with the examination process. In fact, if numerous cases selected for audit result in "no change," there may be a problem with the process for selection of returns for audit, not with the examination results.

Dual status/split duties

A worker may perform services for a single business in two or more separate capacities. A dual status worker performs one type of service for a business as an independent contractor, but performs a different type of service for the business as an employee. *See,* Rev. Rul. 58-505, 1958-2 C.B.728.

Developing the facts

Once you understand the work that is being performed, and the business context in which it is being performed, you need to identify and evaluate evidence. For instance, worker status cannot be determined simply by looking at job titles. Facts must be developed to make a correct determination. When you develop the facts, consider the following:

- In making a determination, you need to look at the entire relationship between a business and a worker. The relationship often has several facets, some indicating the business has control, while others indicate it does not. You will need to weigh this evidence.
- Control is a matter of degree. In fact, even in the clearest case of an independent contractor, the worker is constrained in some way. Conversely, employees may have autonomy in some areas.
- To make a correct determination regarding the status of the worker, you need to consider the evidence of both autonomy and the right to control. The absence of a fact that would indicate control may be as important as its presence.

COMMON LAW EMPLOYEE: CONTROL STANDARD

Important Preliminary points

Important preliminary points can be made:

- There is no "magic number" of relevant evidentiary facts.

- Whatever the number of facts, they should be used in evaluating the extent of the right to direct and control.
- As in any examination, all relevant information needs to be explored and weighed before answering the legal question of whether the right to direct and control associated with an employer-employee relationship exists.
- The evidence that you gather must be factual and well-documented and must support your determination: it is not sufficient to state a legal theory.

A LOOK AT THE EVIDENCE

Categories of evidence

Recognizing that the common law changes the relevancy and emphasis of certain facts over the years, consider types of information which are most persuasive. The following reflects primary categories of evidence and includes examples of key facts that illustrate the right to direct and control—or its absence.

Behavioral Control Facts which illustrate whether there is a right to direct or control how the worker performs the specific task for which he or she is engaged:
- instructions
- training

Financial Control Facts which illustrate whether there is a right to direct or control how the business aspects of the worker's activities are conducted:
- significant investment
- unreimbursed expenses
- services available to the relevant market
- method of payment
- opportunity for profit or loss

Relationship of the Parties Facts which illustrate how the parties perceive their relationship:
- intent of parties/written contracts

- employee benefits
- discharge/termination
- regular business activity

BEHAVIORAL CONTROL

Background

In this section, we consider evidence that substantiates the right to direct or control the details and means by which the worker performs the required services. Training and instructions provided by the business are important in this context. We will also discuss such workplace developments as evaluation systems and concern for customer security in conjunction with business identification.

In considering the types of evidence discussed here, and in the remainder of this training material, remember that ALL relevant information must be considered and weighed to determine whether a worker is an independent contractor or an employee.

Instructions Virtually every business will impose on workers, whether independent contractors or employees, some form of instruction (for example, requiring that the job be performed within specified time frames). This fact alone is not sufficient evidence to determine the worker's status.

As with every relevant fact, the goal is to determine whether the business has retained the right to control the details of a worker's performance or instead has given up its right to control those details. Accordingly, the weight of "instructions" in any case depends on the degree to which instructions apply to how the job gets done rather than to the end result.

BEHAVIORAL CONTROL

Types of instructions

Instructions about how to do the work may cover a wide range of topics, for example:
- when to do the work
- where to do the work
- what tools or equipment to use

- what workers to hire to assist with the work
- where to purchase supplies or services
- what work must be performed by a specified individual (including ability to hire assistants)
- what routines or patterns must be used
- what order or sequence to follow

Prior approval The requirement that a worker obtain approval before taking certain actions is an example of instructions.

BEHAVIORAL CONTROL

Degree of instruction

The degree of instruction depends on the scope of instructions, the extent to which the business retains the right to control the worker's compliance with the instructions, and the effect on the worker in the event of noncompliance.

All these provide useful clues for identifying whether the business keeps control over the manner and means of work performance (leaning toward employee status), or only over a particular product or service (leaning toward independent contractor status).

The more detailed the instructions are that the worker is required to follow, the more control the business exercises over the worker, and the more likely the business retains the right to control the methods by which the worker performs the work. Absence of detail in instructions reflects less control.

BEHAVIORAL CONTROL

Presence of instructions or rules mandated by governmental agencies or industry governing bodies

Although the presence and extent of instructions is important in reaching a conclusion as to whether a business retains the right to direct and control the methods by which a worker performs a job, it is also important to consider the weight to be given those instructions if they are imposed by the business only in compliance with governmental or governing body regulations. If a business requires its workers to comply with rules established by a third party (for example, municipal building codes related to construction), the fact that such rules are imposed by the business should be given little weight in determining the worker's status. However, if the business develops more stringent guidelines for a worker in addition to those imposed by a third party, more weight should be given to these instructions in determining whether the business has retained the right to control the worker.

BEHAVIORAL CONTROL

Instructions by customer

You may find that the customer tells the business that engages the worker how work is to be done. This type of evidence must be evaluated with great care.

If the business passes on the customer's instructions about how to do work as its own, the business has, in essence, adopted the customer's standards as its own. You should not disregard the instructions and standards merely because they originated with the customer.

Suggestions v. instructions

In some cases, a business will state that it does not instruct workers, but merely provides suggestions about how work is to be performed. A suggestion does not constitute the right to direct and control. For example, a dispatcher may suggest avoiding Highway X because of traffic congestion. However, if compliance with the suggestions is mandatory, then the suggestions are, in fact, instructions.

BEHAVIORAL CONTROL

Business identification as instructions

In the past, a requirement that a worker wear a uniform or put a business logo on a vehicle had typically been viewed as the type of instruction consistent with employee status. However, in view of increasing concerns about safety, many businesses now provide customers with some reassurance about the identification of those people gaining access to their homes or workplaces.

As a result, the fact that a worker is required to wear a business uniform or other identification, or is required to place the business's name on the worker's vehicle, does not necessarily indicate that the worker is an employee of the business. If the nature of the worker's occupation is such that the worker must be identified with the business for security purposes, wearing a uniform or placing the business's name on a vehicle is a neutral fact in analyzing whether an employment relationship exists.

Nature of occupation for instructions

The nature of a worker's occupation also affects the degree of direction and control necessary to determine worker status. Highly trained professionals such as doctors, accountants, lawyers, engineers, or computer specialists may require very little, if any, training and/or instruction on how to perform their services. In fact, it may be impossible for the business to instruct the worker on how to perform the services because it may lack the essential knowledge and skills to do so. Generally, such professional workers who are engaged in the pursuit of an independent trade, business, or profession in which they offer their services to the public are independent contractors and not employees. *See*, Treas. Reg. section 31.3121(d)-1(c)(2). Nevertheless, an employer-employee relationship can exist between a business and workers in these occupations. *See*, *James v. Commissioner*, 25 T.C. 1296 (1956).

In analyzing the status of professional workers, evidence of control or autonomy with respect to the financial details of how the task is performed tends to be especially important, as does evidence concerning the relationship of the parties.

BEHAVIORAL CONTROL

Nature of work for instructions

An employment relationship may also exist when the work can be done with a minimal amount of direction and control, such as work done by a stockperson, store clerk, or gas station attendant. The absence of need to control should not be confused with the absence of right to control. The right to control contemplated by Treas. Reg. section 31.3121(d)-1(c)(2) and the common law as an incident of employment requires only such supervision as the nature of the work requires. The key fact to consider is whether the business retains the right to direct and control the worker, regardless of whether the business actually exercises that right.

Evaluation systems

Like instructions, evaluation systems are used by virtually all businesses to monitor the quality of work performed by workers, whether independent contractors or employees. Thus, in analyzing whether a business's evaluation system provides evidence of the right to control work performance or the absence of such a right, you should look for evidence of how the evaluation system may influence the worker's behavior in performing the details of the job. If an evaluation system measures compliance with performance standards concerning the details of how the work is to be performed, the system and its enforcement are evidence of control over the worker's behavior. However, not all businesses have developed formal performance standards or evaluation systems. This is especially true of smaller businesses. The lack of a formal evaluation system is a neutral fact.

BEHAVIORAL CONTROL

Training

Training is a classic means of explaining detailed methods and procedures to be used in performing a task. Periodic or on-going training provided by a business about procedures to be followed and methods to be used indicates that the business wants the services performed in a particular manner. This type of training is strong evidence of an employer-employee relationship. However, not all training rises to this level. The following types of training, which might be provided to either independent contractors or employees, should be disregarded:

- orientation or information sessions about the business's policies, new product line, or applicable statutes or government regulations
- programs that are voluntary and are attended by a worker without compensation

FINANCIAL CONTROL

Economic aspects of relationship
In this section, we consider evidence of whether the business has the right to direct or control the economic aspects of the worker's activities. Economic aspects of the relationship between the parties are frequently analyzed in determining worker status. These illustrate who has financial control of the activities undertaken. The items that usually need to be explored are:
- significant investment
- unreimbursed expenses
- services available to the relevant market
- method of payment
- opportunity for profit or loss

All of these can be thought of as bearing on the issue of whether the recipient has the right to direct and control the means and details of the business aspects of how the worker performs services. The first four items are important in their own right, but also affect whether there is an opportunity for the realization of profit or loss.

Economic dependence
Although economic aspects of the relationship between a worker and a business are significant in determining worker status, it is equally important to understand that some features of the economic relationship are not relevant. The question to be asked is whether the recipient has the right to direct and control business-related means and details of the worker's performance. The question is not whether the worker is economically dependent on or independent of the business for which services are performed. This analysis has been rejected by Congress and the Supreme Court as a basis for determining worker classification.
Nationwide Mutual Insurance Co. v. Darden, 503 U.S. 318 (1992). As a result, the worker's economic status is inappropriate for use in analyzing worker status. Significant investment
A significant investment is evidence that an independent contractor relationship may exist. It should be stressed, however, that a significant

investment is not necessary for independent contractor status. Some types of work simply do not require large expenditures. Further, even if large expenditures (such as costly equipment) are required, an independent contractor may rent the equipment needed at fair rental value.

FINANCIAL CONTROL

No dollar limitation on investment

There are no precise dollar limits that must be met in order to have a significant investment. However, you must be sure that the investment has substance. Further, as long as the worker pays fair market or fair rental value, the worker's relationship to the seller or lessor is irrelevant. The size of the worker's investment and the risk borne by the worker are not diminished merely because the seller or lessor receives the benefit of the worker's services.

Business expenses

The extent to which a worker chooses to incur expenses and bear their costs impacts the worker's opportunity for profit or loss. This constitutes evidence that the worker has the right to direct and control the financial aspects of the business operations. Although not every independent contractor need make a significant investment, almost every independent contractor will incur an array of business expenses either in the form of direct expenditures or in the form of fees for pro rata portions of one or several expenses. These may include:

- and utilities
- tools and equipment
- training
- advertising
- payments to business managers and agents
- wages or salaries of assistants
- licensing/certification/professional dues
- insurance
- postage and delivery
- repairs and maintenance

- supplies
- travel
- leasing of equipment
- depreciation
- inventory/cost of goods sold

Reimbursed expenses

Businesses often pay business or travel expenses for their employees. However, independent contractors' expenses may also be reimbursed. Independent contractors may contract for direct reimbursement of certain expenses or may seek to establish contract prices that will reimburse them for these expenses. You should, therefore, focus on unreimbursed expenses, which better distinguish independent contractors and employees, inasmuch as independent contractors are more likely to have unreimbursed expenses.

Unreimbursed expenses

If expenses are unreimbursed, then the opportunity for profit or loss exists. Fixed ongoing costs that are incurred regardless of whether work is currently being performed are especially important. However, employees may also incur unreimbursed expenses in connection with the services they perform for their businesses. Thus, relatively minor expenses incurred by a worker, or more significant expenses that are customarily borne by an employee in a particular line of business, such as an auto mechanic's tools, would generally not indicate an independent contractor relationship.

Services available

An independent contractor is generally free to seek out business opportunities. Indeed, the independent contractor's economic prosperity depends on doing so successfully. As a result, independent contractors often advertise, maintain a visible business location, and are available to work for the relevant market.

Of course, these activities are not essential for independent contractor status. An independent contractor with special skills may be contacted by word of mouth without the need for advertising. An independent contractor who has negotiated a long-term contract may find advertising equally unnecessary and may be unavailable to work for others for the duration of the contract. Further, other independent contractors may find that a visible business location does not generate sufficient business to justify the expense. Therefore, the absence of these activities is a neutral fact.

Method of payment

The method of payment may be helpful in determining whether the worker has the opportunity for profit or loss.

Salary or hourly wage

A worker who is compensated on an hourly, daily, weekly, or similar basis is guaranteed a return for labor. This is generally evidence of an employer-employee relationship, even when the wage or salary is accompanied by a commission. However, in some lines of business, such as law, it is typical to pay independent contractors on an hourly basis.

Flat fee Performance of a task for a flat fee is generally evidence of an independent contractor relationship, especially if the worker incurs the expenses of performing the services. When payments are made (daily, weekly, or monthly) is not relevant.

Commissions A commission-based worker may be either an independent contractor or employee. The worker's status may depend on the worker's ability to realize a profit or incur a loss as a result of services rendered.

Realization of profit and loss

The ability to realize a profit or incur a loss is probably the strongest evidence that a worker controls the business aspects of services rendered. The facts already considered—significant investment, unreimbursed expenses, making services available, and method of payment—are all relevant in this regard.

As part of this review, you should also consider whether the worker is free to make business decisions which affect the worker's profit or loss. If the worker is making decisions which affect his or her bottom line, the worker likely has the ability to realize profit or loss. Examples include decisions regarding the types and quantities of inventory to acquire, the type and amount of monetary or capital investment, and whether to purchase or lease premises or equipment. Remember that employees can also make these decisions, but they do not usually affect the employee's bottom line. It is sometimes asserted that because a worker can receive more money by working longer hours or receive less money by working less, the worker has the ability to incur a profit or loss. This type of income variation, however, is also consistent with employee status and does not distinguish employees from independent contractors.

Not all facts required

Note that not all financial control facts need be present in order for the worker to have the ability to realize profit or loss. For example, a worker who is paid on a straight commission basis, makes business decisions, and has unreimbursed business expenses likely would have the ability to realize profit or loss—even if the worker does not have a significant investment and does not market services.

RELATIONSHIP OF THE PARTIES

Relationship of business and worker

In this section, we describe other facts that recent court decisions consider relevant in determining worker status. Most of these facts reflect how the worker and the business perceive their relationship to each other. It is much harder to link the facts in this category directly to the right to direct and control how work is to be performed than the categories previously discussed. However, the relationship of the parties is important because it reflects the parties' intent concerning control.

Intent of parties/written contract

Courts often look at the intent of the parties. This is most often embodied in their contractual relationship. Thus, a written agreement describing the worker as an independent contractor is viewed as evidence of the parties' intent that a worker is an independent contractor.

A contractual designation, in and of itself, is not sufficient evidence for determining worker status. The facts and circumstances under which a worker performs services are determinative of the worker's status. Treas. Reg. section 31.3121(d)-1(a)(3) provides that the designation or description of the parties is immaterial. This means that the substance of the relationship, not the label, governs the worker's status. The contract may, however, be relevant in ascertaining methods of compensation, expenses that will be incurred, and the rights and obligations of each party with respect to how work is to be performed.

In addition, if it is difficult, if not impossible, to decide whether a worker is an independent contractor or an employee, the intent of the parties, as reflected in the contractual designation, is an effective way to resolve the issue. The contractual designation of the worker is "very significant in close cases." *See, Illinois Tri-Seal Prods., Inc. v. United States,* 353 F.2d 216, 218 (Ct. Cl. 1965).

Forms W-2 Filing a Form W-2 usually indicates the parties' belief that the worker is an employee. However, workers have succeeded in obtaining independent contractor status even when Forms W-2 were filed. *See, e.g., Butts v. Commissioner,* T.C. Memo 1993-478, *aff'd per curiam* 49 F.3d 713 (11th Cir. 1995).

Incorporation

Questions sometimes arise concerning whether a worker who creates a corporation through which to perform services can be an employee of a business that engages the corporation. Provided that the corporate\formalities are properly followed and at least one non-tax business purpose exists, the corporate form is generally recognized for both state law and federal law, including federal tax, purposes. Disregarding the corporate entity is generally an extraordinary remedy, applied by most courts only in cases of clear abuse. Thus, the worker will usually not be treated as an employee of the business, but as an employee of the corporation. However, the fact that a worker receives payment for services from a business through the worker's corporation does not automatically require a finding of independent contractor status with respect to those services. For example, a professional athlete who attempted to assign a salary received from the team to a wholly-owned professional corporation was nevertheless held by the Tax Court to be a common law employee of the team, rather than the professional corporation. *Sargent v. Commissioner*, 93 T.C. 572 (1989), *rev'd* 929 F.2d 1252 (8th Cir. 1991). *Sargent's* reversal by the Eighth Circuit illustrates courts' reluctance to disregard the corporate entity. *See, Leavell v. Commissioner*, 104 T.C. 140 (January 30, 1995).

Employee benefits

Providing a worker with employee benefits traditionally associated with employee status has been an important fact in several recent court decisions. *See, Weber v. Commissioner, supra; Lewis v. Commissioner*, T.C. Memo 1993-635. If a worker receives employee benefits, such as paid vacation days, paid sick days, health insurance, life or disability insurance, or a pension, this constitutes some evidence of employee status. The evidence is strongest if the worker is provided with employee benefits under a tax-qualified retirement plan, IRC section 403(b) annuity, or cafeteria plan, for, by statute, these employee benefits can ONLY be provided to employees. Some decisions, however, have ascribed less weight to the fact that employee benefits were provided. *See, e.g., Butts v. Commissioner, supra*.

If a worker is excluded from a benefit plan because the worker is not considered an employee by the business, this is relevant (though not conclusive) in determining the worker's status as an independent contractor.

In contrast, if the worker is excluded on some other grounds (*e.g.*, the worker's work location or business unit), the exclusion is irrelevant in determining whether the worker is an independent contractor or an employee. This is because none of these employee benefits is required to be provided to employees. Many workers whose status as bona fide employees is unquestioned receive no employee benefits. This pattern is possible even if some workers in a business receive employee benefits, for there is no requirement that all workers be covered.

State law characterization

State laws, or determinations of state or federal agencies, may characterize a worker as an employee for purposes of various benefits. Characterizations based on these laws or determinations should be disregarded, because the laws or regulations involved may use different definitions of employee or be interpreted to achieve particular policy objectives.

For example, state laws determine whether workers are employees for purposes of workers' compensation and unemployment insurance. Because the definition of "employee" for these purposes is often broader than under the common law rules, eligibility for these benefits should be disregarded in determining worker status.

Discharge/termination

The circumstances under which a business or a worker can terminate their relationship have traditionally been considered useful evidence bearing on the status the parties intended the worker to have.

Some recent court decisions continue to explore such evidence. However, in order to determine whether the facts before you are relevant to the worker's status, you will need to consider the impact of modern business practices and legal standards governing worker termination.

Discharge/termination—
Traditional analysis

Under a traditional analysis, a business's ability to terminate the work relationship at will, without penalty, provided a highly effective method to control the details of how work was performed and, therefore, tended to indicate employee status. Conversely, in the traditional independent contractor relationship, the business could terminate the relationship only if the worker failed to provide the intended product or service, thus indicating the parties' intent that the business not have the right to control how the work was performed.

Limits on ability to discharge worker

In practice, however, businesses rarely have complete flexibility in discharging an employee. The business may be liable for pay in lieu of notice, severance pay, "golden parachutes," or other forms of compensation when it discharges an employee. In addition, the reasons for which a business can terminate an employee may be limited—whether by law, by contract, or by its own practices. As a result, inability to freely discharge a worker, by itself, no longer constitutes persuasive evidence that the worker is an independent contractor.

Limits on worker's ability to quit

Looking at the issue from the other angle, a worker's ability to terminate work at will was traditionally considered to illustrate that the worker merely provided labor and tended to indicate an employer-employee relationship. In contrast, if the worker terminated work, and the business could refuse payment or sue for nonperformance, this indicated the business's interest in receipt of the product or service for which the parties had contracted and tended to indicate an independent contractor relationship.

Termination of contracts

In practice, however, independent contractors may enter into short-term contracts for which nonperformance remedies are inappropriate or may negotiate limits on their liability for nonperformance. For example, professionals, such as doctors and attorneys, are typically able to terminate their contractual relationship without penalty.

Nonperformance by employee

At the same time, businesses may successfully sue employees for substantial damages resulting from their failure to perform the services for which they were engaged. As a result, the presence or absence of limits on a worker's ability to terminate the relationship, by themselves, no longer constitutes useful evidence in determining worker status. On the other hand, a business's ability to refuse payment for unsatisfactory work continues to be characteristic of an independent contractor relationship.

Discharge/termination –limited usefulness

Because the significance of facts bearing on the right to discharge/terminate is so often unclear and depends primarily on contract and labor law, this type of evidence should be used with great caution.

Permanency

Courts have considered the existence of a permanent relationship between the worker and the business as relevant evidence in determining whether there is an employer-employee relationship.

Indefinite relationship

If a business engages a worker with the expectation that the relationship will continue indefinitely, rather than for a specific project or period, this is generally considered evidence of their intent to create an employment relationship.

Long-term relationship

However, a relationship that is created with the expectation that it will be indefinite should not be confused with a long-term relationship. A long-term relationship may exist between a business and either an independent contractor or an employee.

The relationship between the business and an independent contractor may be long-term for several reasons:
- the contract may be a long-term contract
- contracts may be renewed regularly due to superior service, competitive costs, or lack of alternative service providers A business may also have a relationship with an employee that is long-term, but not indefinite. This could occur if temporary employment contracts are renewed or if a long-term, but not indefinite, employment contract is entered into. As a result, a relationship that is long-term, but not indefinite, is a neutral fact that should be disregarded.

Temporary relationship

A temporary relationship is also a neutral fact that should be weighed carefully. An independent contractor will typically have a temporary relationship with a business, but so too will employees engaged on a seasonal, project, or "as needed" basis.

Regular business activity

The courts have looked at the services performed by the worker and the extent to which those services are a key aspect of the regular business of the company.

In considering this evidentiary fact, you should remember that the mere fact that a service is desirable, necessary, or even essential to a business does not mean that the service provider is an employee. An appliance store needs workers to install electricity and plumbing in the store building. However, this work can be done equally well by independent contractors or employees.

In this case, you can avoid confusion by focusing on the fact that the work the electricians and plumbers perform in the store is not the store's regular business.

In contrast, the work of an attorney or paralegal is part of the regular business of a law firm. If a law firm hires an attorney or paralegal, it is likely that it will present their work as its own. As a result, there is an increased probability that the law firm will direct or control their activities.

However, you need to examine further facts to see whether there is evidence of the right to direct or control before you conclude that these workers are employees. It is possible that the work performed is part of the principal business of the law firm, yet it has hired workers who are outside specialists and may be independent contractors.

FACTS OF LESSER IMPORTANCE

Introduction

This section discusses facts that will typically provide less useful evidence of whether a worker is an independent contractor or an employee. In past decades, these facts were probably more important. However, recent court decisions give them little independent weight. To the extent these facts continue to have relevance, they are generally already reflected in the types of evidence described previously.

Part-time or fulltime work

The fact that a worker performed services on a part-time basis or worked for more than one person or business was once thought to be significant evidence indicating that the worker was an independent contractor. However, in today's economy, whether a worker performs services on a fulltime or part-time basis is a neutral fact. There are several reasons for this change. With cutbacks and downsizing in business and industry, many companies hire workers on a part-time basis. These workers may be either independent contractors or employees.

Similarly, working full-time for one business is also consistent with either independent contractor or employee status. An independent contractor may work full-time for one business either because other contracts are lacking, because the contract by its terms requires a full-time, exclusive effort, or because the independent contractor chooses to devote full-time to a particular project.

Finally, many employees "moonlight" by working for a second employer. As a result, whether services are performed for one business is no longer useful evidence.

Place of work

Whether work is performed on the business's premises or at a location selected by the business often has no bearing on worker status. Even when it is relevant evidence, it will be relevant because it illustrates the business's right to direct and control how the work is performed and will have been considered in connection with instructions.

One location

In many cases, services can be provided at only one location. For example, repairing a leaky pipe requires a plumber to visit the premises where the pipe is located. Similarly, a camera operator must shoot a commercial at the same location as the director and actors. These requirements are inherent in the result to be achieved and are not evidence of the right to direct and control how the work is performed.

Different locations

In other cases, work can be performed at many different locations. Modern technology has developed tools that greatly expand the scope of the workplace, such as cellular phones, modems, and computer networks. Allowing work offsite can be attractive to businesses due to lowering costs, improving morale, and helping to retain valued workers. In today's world, off-site work is consistent with either an independent contractor or employer-employee relationship.

The place where work is performed is most likely to be relevant evidence in cases in which the worker has an office or other business location. However, you will have already considered this evidence in evaluating significant investment, unreimbursed expenses, and opportunity for profit or loss.

Hours of work

You can easily apply the same reasoning that we used in connection with place of work to understand why hours of work is also a fact that, if relevant, has already been considered in connection with instructions. Some work must, by its nature, be performed at a specific time. Again, our camera operator must be ready to provide photography services when the director and actors are on hand. This relates to the result to be achieved, not how the work is performed. Modern communications have increased the ease of performing work outside normal business hours, while flexibility in setting hours may improve morale and retain valued workers. In today's world, flexible hours are consistent with either independent contractor or employee status.

WEIGHING THE EVIDENCE

Control and autonomy both present

When you have explored the relevant evidence, you will probably find some facts that support independent contractor status and other facts that support employee status. This is because independent contractors are rarely totally unconstrained in the performance of their contracts, while employees almost always have some degree of autonomy. Which predominates?

You will, therefore, need to weigh the evidence before you in order to determine whether, looking at the relationship as a whole, evidence of control or autonomy predominates. You may, for example, find that the business requires the worker to be on site during normal business hours, but has no right to control other aspects of how the work is to be performed; that the worker has a substantial investment and unreimbursed expenses combined with a flat fee payment; and that contractual provisions clearly show the parties' intent that the worker be an independent contractor. In this case, you would logically conclude that the worker was an independent contractor despite the instructions about the hours and place of work.

SUMMARY

Review of lesson The following summarizes what we have covered in this lesson:

1. In determining a worker's status, you should gain an understanding of the way a business operates and the relationship between the business and the worker.
2. Areas to consider while developing your case are:
   - What the business does and how the job gets done.
   - The relationship between the business and its clients or customers.
   - Facts that indicate whether the business has the right to control how work is done.
3. Evidence that may be the most persuasive can be identified within three specific categories.
   - Behavioral control.
   - Financial control.
   - Relationship of the parties.
4. Behavioral control focuses on whether there is a right to direct or control how the work is done. The presence or absence of instructions and training on how work is to be done are especially relevant.
5. Financial control focuses on whether there is a right to direct or control how the business aspects of the worker's activities are conducted. Significant investment, unreimbursed expenses, services available to the relevant market, method of payment, and opportunity for profit or loss are facts relevant to financial control.
6. Relationship of the parties focuses on how the parties perceive their relationship. Intent of parties/written contract, employee benefits,

discharge/termination, permanency, and regular business activity are relevant to how the parties perceive their relationship.
7. Relevant evidence in all three categories must be weighed to determine the worker's status.

SELECTED CASES

United States v. Silk, 331 U.S. 704 (1947)
In this case, the Supreme Court applied the common law standard in concluding that the coal unloaders at issue were employees, whereas the coal truck and moving van drivers were independent contractors. However, the Court also suggested that the meaning of the term "employee" should be given a broader meaning in order to carry out the purpose of social security legislation. For history of repudiation of this broader meaning, *see, Illinois Tri-Seal* below.

Bartels v. Birmingham, 332 U.S. 126 (1947)
The Supreme Court applied the common law standard in determining that band members were employees of the bandleader, rather than of dance hall operators. However, the Court also suggested that an "economic reality" test should be used for purposes of interpreting the social security legislation.
For history of the repudiation of the "economic reality" test, *see, Illinois Tri-Seal* below.

Illinois Tri-Seal Products v. United States, 353 F.2d 216 (Ct. Cl. 1965) An excellent history of the Congressional repudiation of the *Silk/Bartels* "economic reality" approach can be found in this case holding window installers to be independent contractors. The case also illustrates the intrinsically factual nature of independent contractor/employee determinations. It also contains helpful discussions of the distinction between instructions and suggestions and of the significance of the parties' view of their relationship in close cases.

McGuire v. United States, 349 F.2d 644 (9th Cir. 1965)

This case, holding "swampers" who unloaded produce trucks to be employees, distinguishes between the right to control and the need to control in the context of workers requiring little supervision.
Avis Rent-A-Car System, Inc. v. United States, 503 F.2d 423 (2d Cir. 1974)
The importance of avoiding single fact analysis is stressed in this case holding car shuttlers to be employees. Facts considered relevant include the right to control the manner in which work is performed, substantial investment, expenses, ability to profit, special skills, permanence, and whether work is part of the principal's regular business. *Simpson v. Commissioner*, 64 T.C. 974 (1975)
The IRS successfully argued in this case that an insurance agent was an independent contractor. Relevant facts were: 1) degree of control over details; 2) investment in facilities; 3) opportunity for profit or loss; 4) right to discharge; 5) whether work is part of principal's regular business; 6) permanency; and 7) the relationship the parties believed they were creating.
Professional and Executive Leasing, Inc. v. Commissioner, 862 F.2d 751 (9th Cir. 1988). *James v. Commissioner*, 25 T.C. 1296 (1956)
Both cases focus on the right to control the manner in which the work of highly skilled professionals is performed.
Nationwide Mutual Insurance Co. v. Darden, 503 U.S. 318 (1992)
In this case under Title I of the Employee Retirement Income Security Act of 1974 (ERISA), the Supreme Court held that traditional common law concepts should be used to interpret the term "employee" absent legislative direction to the contrary. The decision contains the Supreme Court's repudiation of the "economic reality" dicta in *Silk*. *Weber v. Commissioner*, 103 T.C. 378 (1994), *aff'd per curiam* 60 F.3d 1104 (4th Cir. 1995). *Shelley v. Commissioner*, T.C. Memo 1994-432.
The importance of small factual differences is apparent in these two cases. In *Weber*, a Methodist minister was held to be an employee, while in *Shelley*, a clergyman in another denomination was held to be an independent contractor.

STATUTORY EMPLOYEES, STATUTORY NON-EMPLOYEES, AND OTHER CLASSES OF WORKERS INTRODUCTION

In this lesson In the previous lesson, you studied what constitutes a common law employee where the business is liable for FICA, FUTA, and federal income tax withholding. In this lesson, you will study corporate officers and certain workers that are defined by statute as employees, commonly referred to as "statutory employees." You will also study workers in three occupations where, by statute, the worker performing the services is specifically not treated as an employee (commonly referred to as "statutory non-employee"). In cases of a statutory non-employee, the business for which the services are performed is not treated as an employer, and, therefore, is not liable for any of these taxes. IRC section 3121(d) contains four categories of employees for FICA tax purposes:

- common law employees
- corporate officers
- statutory employees
- employees covered by an agreement under section 218 of the Social Security Act IRC section 3508 contains tests for the treatment of real estate agents and direct sellers as statutory non-employees. IRC section 3506 provides the requirements for treating companion sitters as statutory non-employees.

Objectives At the end of this lesson, you will be able to:
1. Determine whether a corporate officer is an employee for purposes of FICA and FUTA taxes and federal income tax withholding.
2. Identify statutory employees for purposes of FICA and FUTA taxes.
3. Identify statutory non-employees.

CORPORATE OFFICERS

Exception Officers are specifically included within the definition of employee for purposes of FICA, FUTA, and federal income tax withholding. See IRC sections 3121(d)(1), 3306(i), and 3401(c). The common law standard is not applicable. The regulations provide that generally an officer of a corporation is an employee of the corporation. However, an officer is not considered to be an employee of the corporation if two requirements are met: (1) the officer does not perform any services or performs only minor services; and (2) the officer is not entitled to receive, directly or indirectly, any remuneration. Treas. Reg. section 31.3121(d)-1(b). The officer must meet both requirements to be excepted from employee status. In determining whether services performed by a corporate officer are considered minor or nominal, examine the character of the service, the frequency and duration of performance, and the actual or potential importance or necessity of the services in relation to the conduct of the corporation's business.

A director of a corporation, acting in the capacity of a director, is not an employee of the corporation for those services, even if that worker also serves as an employee or officer of the corporation for other services. Therefore, part of the compensation paid this worker can be for services rendered as an independent contractor (director) and part of the payments can be for services rendered as an employee. Rev. Rul. 58-505.

EXAMPLE

Various officers of five related operating corporations performed only minor ministerial functions entailing a few hours work a year for the corporations. The officers also received no remuneration for the services they performed for these five corporations. Because the officers satisfied both requirements for the exception from employee status (*i.e.*, they performed only minor services for the corporations and received no remuneration), the officers were not employees of the operating corporations. Rev. Rul. 74-390, 1974-2 C.B. 331.

However, the sole shareholder of a closely held corporation performing services as a corporate officer, who either performs more than minor services or receives compensation for the services, is an employee even though the services performed and the amount of compensation for them are under the sole shareholder officer's complete control. Rev. Rul. 71-86, 1971-1 C.B. 285.

Payments to officers

You should closely examine all payments to the officer, such as amounts labeled as draws, loans, dividends, or other distributions, to determine whether the payments are in fact wages for FICA, FUTA, and federal income tax withholding purposes. For example, in Rev. Rul. 74-44, 1974-1 C.B. 287, the two shareholders of an S corporation received no compensation for services they performed for the corporation. Instead, they arranged to receive "dividends" from the corporation. The ruling concluded that the dividends were in fact compensation for services and were wages for purposes of FICA, FUTA, and federal income tax withholding.

STATUTORY EMPLOYEES

Statutory employee

If a worker is not an employee under the usual common law rules or a corporate officer, the worker and the business may nevertheless still be subject to employment taxes. IRC section 3121(d)(3) lists workers in four occupational groups who, under certain circumstances, are considered employees for FICA tax, and, in some instances, FUTA tax, but not for federal income tax withholding. These groups include:

- agent-drivers or commission-drivers
- full-time life insurance salespersons
- home workers
- traveling or city salespersons

These workers are referred to as "statutory employees." Workers in these four occupational groups are employees for FICA tax purposes. By definition, a worker cannot be a statutory employee under IRC section 3121(d)(3) if that worker is a common law employee. *See Lickiss v. Commissioner*, T.C. Memo 1994-103.

General requirements

In order for IRC section 3121(d)(3) to apply when a worker performs services for remuneration for a business, there are three general requirements. They are:

1. The contract of service contemplates that the worker will personally perform substantially all the work.

2. The worker has no substantial investment in facilities other than transportation facilities used in performing the work.
3. There is a continuing work relationship with the business for which the services are performed.

Work performed personally

The term "contract of service" means an arrangement oral or written, under which the particular services are performed. The term "personally perform" means it is contemplated that the worker will do substantially all the work personally. Therefore, if the arrangement contemplates that the worker would be free to delegate as much of the work as he or she desires, then the worker could not be a statutory employee under this section.

No substantial investment

The term "substantial investment" is not defined in the regulations. All of the facts for each case must be considered to determine whether the facilities furnished by the worker are substantial. Several factors listed below should be considered:

1. What is the value of the worker's investment compared to the total investment?
2. Are the facilities furnished essential to perform the work or for the personal convenience of the worker?
3. Are the facilities being purchased or leased at fair market or fair rental value?
4. Are the facilities furnished by the worker considerably more extensive than those usually furnished by workers performing comparable services?

Continuing relationship

Work is considered to be of a continuing nature if it is regular or frequently recurring. Regular part-time and regular seasonal work are considered continuing. A single job transaction is not generally a continuing relationship.

CATEGORIES OF STATUTORY EMPLOYEES

Agent drivers or commission drivers

The statute limits agent drivers or commission drivers to workers who distribute meat or meat products, vegetables or vegetable products, fruit or fruit products, bakery products, beverages (other than milk), or laundry or dry-cleaning services for a business. The distribution of other services or products will not disqualify the worker from this category of statutory employee if handling the additional products or services is incidental to handling the specified items. The agent or commission drivers may sell at retail or wholesale. They may operate from their own trucks or from trucks belonging to the business for which they work. The drivers may serve customers designated by the business as well as those they solicit. Their compensation may be based on commission, or the difference between the price charged to the customer and the price paid by the driver to the business for the product or service.

Full-time life insurance salespersons

This group includes salespersons whose full-time occupation is soliciting life insurance or annuity contracts or both, primarily for one life insurance business.

Generally, the contract of employment reflects the intent of the worker and the business in determining whether the worker is a full-time or part-time salesperson. The actual time devoted to the work is not determinative. A worker may work regularly only a few hours each day and still qualify as a full-time life insurance salesperson.

The salesperson's efforts must be devoted primarily to soliciting life insurance or annuity contracts. Occasional or incidental sales of other types of insurance for the business, or the occasional placing of surplus-line insurance, will not affect this requirement. However, the salesperson who devotes substantial efforts to selling applications for insurance contracts other than life insurance and annuity contracts (for example, health and accident, fire, automobile, etc.) does not meet the requirement.

Home workers The term "home worker" can encompass workers who perform a wide range of duties. Traditionally, this group would have included, but was not limited to, workers who would make such things as clothing, bedding, needlecraft products, or similar products. In addition, it can also include workers who provide typing or transcribing services. *See* Rev. Rul. 64-280, 1964-2 C.B. 384 and Rev. Rul. 70-340, 1970-1 C.B. 202. The work is done away from the business's place of business, usually in the worker's own home, the home of another, or a home workshop.

Specific requirements for home workers

To qualify as a statutory employee, the worker must meet, in addition to the three general requirements previously listed, the following requirements:

1. The work must be done in accordance with the specifications given by the business (generally, simple and consisting of such things as patterns or samples).
2. The material or goods on which the work is done must be furnished by the business.
3. The finished product must be returned to the business or to another designation. It is immaterial whether the business picks up the work, or the worker delivers it.

$100 rule for home workers

$100 Rule—IRC section 3121(a)(10) provides that the pay which the home worker receives for such work is not subject to FICA tax unless $100 or more of cash (checks, money orders, or cashiers checks) is received during any calendar year from one business. A home worker may be employed by several businesses.

If the $100 cash pay test is met, all non-cash payments (clothes, merchandise, transportation passes, etc.) from the same business are also included as wages.

Traveling or city salesperson

This category includes workers who operate away from the business's premises. Their full-time business activity is selling merchandise for a business. The test of full-time relates to an exclusive or principal business activity for a single business and not to the time spent on a job. Sideline sales activities for some other business, however, do not exclude these workers from coverage.

Specific requirements for traveling or city salespersons

In order for traveling or city salespersons to fall within the statutory test, they must meet, in addition to the three general requirements previously listed, the following requirements:

1. Their entire or principal business activity must be devoted to soliciting and transmitting orders for merchandise of a single business.
2. The orders must be obtained from wholesalers, retailers, contractors, or operators of hotels, restaurants, or other similar establishments.
3. The merchandise sold must be bought for resale or must be supplied for use in the purchaser's business operations.

Principal business activity defined for traveling or city salespersons

The definition of an entire or principal business activity is discussed in Rev. Rul. 55-31, 1955-1 C.B. 476. Generally, the test is met if 80 percent of the activity is for one business.

Types of purchasers for traveling or city salespersons

Workers must sell principally to the classes of purchasers described in IRC section 3121(d)(3)(D) to be considered statutory employees. They may also sell incidentally to others.

CLASS OF PURCHASER DESCRIPTION

Wholesaler A wholesaler buys merchandise in large quantities and usually sells in small quantities to jobbers or to retail dealers but not to the ultimate consumer. The wholesaler does not process the merchandise in any way to cause it to lose or change its identity. Retailer A retailer buys merchandise in small quantities and then sells it in smaller quantities usually to the ultimate consumer. Retail establishments may perform service functions or processing or manufacturing operations with respect to the items they sell without losing their character as retail establishments. For example, a store which sells drapery and slip cover material, and also makes draperies and slip covers for the consumer, is a retail establishment and not a manufacturer. A neighborhood bakery is essentially a retail store, even though it changes the form of the raw material to the final prepared material. Contractors include such service organizations as contractors for window washing, wall cleaning, construction, and other services.

Hotels, Restaurants, or Other Similar Establishments

The phrase "other similar establishments" refers solely to establishments similar to hotels and restaurants whose primary function is the furnishing of food or lodging.

Classes of purchasers not included for traveling or city salespersons

Manufacturers, schools, hospitals, churches, municipalities, and state and federal governments are not within the included classes of purchasers. A manufacturer produces articles for use from raw or prepared materials by giving them new forms, qualities, and properties, or combinations of these items. Sales made to a unit of an organization not within the included classes of purchasers may meet the requirements regarding "classes of purchasers" provided the unit carries on a separate and clearly identifiable business with a type of purchaser described in IRC section 3121(d)(3)(D). For example, sales made to an unincorporated university bookstore, owned and operated by the university, are sales made to a purchaser included in the statutory definition of "traveling or city salesperson."

Resale or use for traveling or city salespersons

Merchandise must be for resale or for use in the business operation of the purchaser. The phrase "merchandise for resale" includes only tangibles which do not lose their identity as they pass through the hands of the purchaser. The phrase "supplies for use in the business operation" means principally supplies used in conducting the purchaser's business. This includes all tangible merchandise not considered "merchandise for resale." Services, such as radio time and advertising space, are intangible and outside the definition. However, items such as advertising novelties and calendars constitute supplies within the definition.

Service may be part of the sale for traveling or city salespersons

If workers perform substantial work in servicing the articles they sell, they may still meet the requirements of IRC section 3121(d)(3)(D). For example, a worker who spends a day selling a machine and a day supervising its installation and training the purchaser's personnel in its use may still have performed services as a full-time salesperson. Furnishing such services may be a necessary part of the inducement for the buyer to purchase. The question, therefore, is whether the total activity is essentially a selling activity. If so, the services related to the sale, even though substantial, are an integral part of the sale.

Statutory employees' expenses

Statutory employees under IRC section 3121(d)(3) are not employees for the purpose of deducting trade or business expenses. Therefore, they may deduct their expenses on Schedule C rather than as miscellaneous itemized deductions. Rev. Rul. 90-93, 1990-2 C.B. 33. Statutory employees receive a Form W-2. A check is made in Box 15 to indicate that the worker is a statutory employee. Federal income tax withholding does not apply to statutory employees. If statutory employees also have earnings from self-employment, they may not use expenses from services as a statutory employee to reduce net earnings from self-employment for purposes of SECA, IRC section 1402(a). This is because services as a statutory employee do not constitute the carrying on of a trade or business for purposes of SECA. Statutory employees are required to file a Schedule C for services performed as a statutory employee separate from a Schedule C that reports net earnings from self-employment.

Statutory employee treatment

Recently, workers who were otherwise common law employees have claimed to be statutory employees to be eligible for the treatment of Rev. Rul. 90-93. The issue in Rev. Rul. 90-93 was whether a full-time life insurance salesperson who was treated as an employee for FICA purposes under IRC section 3121(d)(3) was also an employee for purposes of IRC sections 62 (relating to above the line deductions) and 67 (relating to two percent floor on miscellaneous itemized deductions). The holding was that a full-time life insurance salesperson described in IRC section 3121(d)(3) is not an employee for purposes of sections 62 and 67. Rev. Rul. 90-93 also applied to all other statutory employees described in IRC section 3121(d)(3) in connection with expenses they incur in the conduct of their trades or businesses.

If a worker's return appears to take inconsistent positions, further evaluation is appropriate. For example, if a worker's return includes a W-2 indicating employee status yet claims deductions related to this income on Schedule C, you should ask the worker for an explanation of the potentially inconsistent positions. If the worker is not a statutory employee, the appropriate adjustment should be made.

Remember, the worker can be a statutory employee only if the worker is an independent contractor under the common law standard.

Statutory employee benefit plans

Except for full-time life insurance salespersons, statutory employees under IRC section 3121(d)(3) remain independent contractors for employee benefit purposes. Thus, they are not eligible to participate in the employee benefit plans sponsored by the business for employees and cannot enjoy the exclusions from income for amounts paid under accident and health insurance arrangements under IRC sections 104, 105, and 106 to the extent that those income tax exclusions apply only to employees. However, statutory employees can establish and maintain their own self-employed retirement plans. Full-time life insurance salespersons are an exception. They are treated as employees not only for FICA tax purposes, but also for certain employee benefit programs maintained by the business. IRC section 7701(a)(20). Thus, they may participate as employees under the business's group term life insurance program under IRC section 79, apply the exclusions available to employees participating in the business's accident and health plans under IRC sections 104, 105, and 106, apply the exclusion from income under IRC section 101(b) for employer provided death benefits, and participate as an employee in the business's qualified deferred compensation or retirement plans under IRC section 401(a) and the business's cafeteria plan under IRC section 125. On the other hand, a full-time life insurance salesperson may not base contributions to a self-employed retirement plan (commonly called a Keogh plan) on the compensation received from the insurance business.

STATE AND LOCAL GOVERNMENT EMPLOYEES
218 Agreement
IRC section 3121(d)(4) provides that workers for state and local governments are employees for FICA purposes if the governmental unit has entered into an agreement with the Social Security Administration to provide FICA coverage pursuant to Section 218 of the Social Security Act. These agreements may be broad or may deal with very specific worker groups. Since April 20, 1983, coverage under a 218 agreement cannot be terminated. Can be employees for FICA purposes under common law. As a result of legislative changes since 1986, workers for state and local governments can also be employees for FICA purposes if they are employees under the common law rules, even though the worker's services are not covered under a Section 218 Agreement. In analyzing how workers who are not covered under a Section 218 Agreement are treated, it is helpful to keep in mind that FICA taxes consist of two components, Old Age, Survivors, and Disability Insurance (OASDI) and Hospital Insurance (Medicare). For services performed after July 1, 1991, both the OASDI and the Medicare components of FICA apply to state and local government common law employees, unless the employee is covered by a public retirement system. As most of these governments have broad coverage in their public retirement systems, relatively few state and local government employees are covered by this rule. The Medicare portion of FICA taxes applies to wages of state and local government common law employees hired after March 31, 1986, unless the employee meets the continuing employment exception of IRC section 3121(u)(2)(C).

STATUTORY NON-EMPLOYEES
Introduction Workers in three occupations will not be treated as employees for FICA, FUTA, or federal income tax withholding purposes provided they meet certain qualifications. These workers are referred to as "statutory non-employees." IRC section 3508 provides that, for all IRC purposes, qualified real estate agents and direct sellers are statutory non-employees. IRC section 3506 provides that, for purposes of subtitle C of

the IRC relating to employment tax, (FICA and FUTA taxes, and federal income tax withholding), qualifying companion sitters are statutory non-employees.

Qualified real estate agents

IRC section 3508 provides that a worker is a qualified real estate agent if the following requirements are met:
1. The worker is a licensed real estate agent.
2. Substantially all of such worker's remuneration for services is directly related to sales or other output rather than to the number of hours worked.
3. A written contract exists between the worker and the business for which services are being performed that provides that the worker will not be treated as an employee for federal tax purposes.

Proposed Treas. Reg. section 31.3508-1(b)(2) defines services performed as a real estate agent and provides examples. Services do not include management of property.

Direct sellers IRC section 3508 provides that a worker is a direct seller if the following qualifications are met:
1. The worker is engaged in the sale of consumer products in the home or in other than a permanent retail establishment.
2. Substantially all of such worker's remuneration for services is directly related to sales or other output rather than the number of hours worked.
3. A written contract exists between the worker and the business for which the services are being performed that provides that the worker will not be treated as an employee for federal tax purposes.

The proposed regulations drafted for IRC section 3508 include detailed explanations of the terms used to define "direct seller." Since their publication in 1986, the regulations have come under increasing criticism. One area that has been attacked concerns the definition of "consumer products." Proposed Treas. Reg. section 31.3508-1(g)(3) defines "consumer products" as tangible personal property used for personal, family, or household purposes, including property intended to be attached to, or installed in any real property.

Litigation of definition of consumer products

The definition of "consumer products" was litigated in *Cleveland Institute of Electronics, Inc.*, 787 F.Supp. 741 (DC. ND. Ohio 1992). In this case, the products being sold were home study educational courses. The Service deemed these courses to be intangible in nature and consequently held that they did not meet the proposed regulations' definition of "consumer products." The District Court's consideration of this matter resulted in the conclusion that the proposed regulations' definition of "consumer products" was unnecessarily restrictive. In deciding that the workers selling these courses were independent contractors, the court expanded the definition to include not only tangible consumer goods, but also intangible consumer services such as the courses at issue.

Consumer products definition expanded

This expanded definition of "consumer products" was subsequently cited in *The R Corporation*, 94-2 USTC par. 50,380 (DC. M.D. FL (1994)) where sellers of TV cable services were involved. In ruling that the sellers of cable service were direct sellers under IRC section 3508, the court concluded that the cable service being sold was an intangible consumer product. Based upon the litigation cited above, and pending finalization of the regulations and further consideration of this issue in that context, cases should not be developed based on a distinction between tangible and intangible products; *i.e.*, both types of products will qualify. In your consideration of direct seller cases, care should be taken, therefore, to ensure that your research is current.

Newspaper carriers and distributors

The Small Business Job Protection Act added qualifying newspaper distributors and carriers as direct sellers. Under the amendment, a person engaged in the trade or business of the delivery or distribution of newspapers or shopping news qualifies as a direct seller provided all remuneration is directly related to sales or output, rather than hours worked. Also, the services must be performed pursuant to a written contract that provides the person will not be treated as an employee for Federal tax purposes. The provision is effective with respect to services performed after December 31, 1995.

Companion sitters

IRC section 3506 provides that a companion sitter will not be an employee of a companion sitting placement service if the companion sitting placement service neither pays nor receives the salary or wages of the sitter. The placement service may be compensated on a fee basis by either the sitter or the person or business for which the sitting is performed.

The companion sitter is deemed to be self-employed unless considered to be a statutory or common law employee of the person or business for which the services are performed. Treas. Reg. section 31-3506-1(c) and (d).

SUMMARY

Review of lesson The following summarizes what we have covered in this lesson:

1. Officers of corporations are employees for purposes of FICA, FUTA, and federal income tax withholding unless the services rendered are minor or nominal, and they neither receive nor are entitled to receive any compensation.
2. Certain classes of workers who do not meet the common law rules of determining employer-employee relationships are still employees for FICA tax purposes. These statutory employees are:
   - Agent or commission drivers.
   - Full-time life insurance salespersons.
   - Home workers.
   - Traveling or city salespersons.
3. Before a worker in one of these four categories is considered a statutory employee, three general requirements must be met: Contract of service states that the work will be performed personally. Worker

has no substantial investment in facilities. Continuing relationship exists between the worker and the business.

4. In determining whether a worker is an employee, first apply the common law rules. If the facts do not support a position that a worker is a common law employee, then apply a test to determine if the worker is a statutory employee. If you determine that a statutory employee situation exists, the business is liable for FICA tax. The business may also be liable for FUTA tax. Remember, the determination that a worker is a statutory employee is made for employment tax purposes. Thus, the worker is not subject to federal income tax withholding and is not eligible for voluntary federal income tax withholding because the common law status is that of independent contractor, not employee.

5. Qualified real estate agents, direct sellers, including newspaper carriers and distributors, and companion sitters are statutory nonemployees and are not treated as employees for purposes of FICA, FUTA, and federal income tax withholding if they meet certain IRC requirements.

CHAPTER 21

AUTHOR'S BIOGRAPHY

SHELDON R. WAXMAN
BOX 309, SOUTH HAVEN, MI 49090-0309
(269) 207-6219 (269) 637-2922—FAX
E-MAIL: shelly@cybersol.com or shelly@thelawyer.info
WEBSITE www.thelawyer.info

PERSONAL:
- Born: Chicago, Illinois, April 22, 1941.
- Married: Katherine.

- Children: Josiah (25) and Zoe (21).
- Residence: South Haven, Michigan

EDUCATION:
- University of Illinois, B.A. (1963). I Majored in Political Science and had a split Minor in Philosophy and Comparative Religion—these are subjects which I followed through my life's path and, also, an ever-abiding interest in American History and Economics;
- DePaul University College of Law, J.D. (1965). SCHOLASTIC HONOR: Member, Blue Key National Honor Fraternity. ACADEMIC HONOR: Casenote Editor, DePaul Law Review.
- <u>Post-College:</u> Advanced Diplomate, Court Practice Institute of Chicago.

BAR ADMISSIONS
- United States Supreme Court (1976),
- Courts of Appeal for 6th, 7th, 9th and 10th Circuits,
- Trial Bar-U.S. District Court for the Northern District of Illinois,
- U.S. District Court for the Western District of Michigan,
- U.S. Tax Court,
- Supreme Courts of Illinois (1965) and Michigan (1985).

SPECIALIZED BACKGROUND
- Member, Employment Tax Committee of the Tax Section of the American Bar Association,
- Member, Tax Section, Michigan Bar Association,
- Member, Tax Freedom Institute,
- Former Trustee in Bankruptcy,
- Federal Defender Panel Member (Chicago and Grand Rapids),
- Executive Club of Chicago Reception Committee,
- Appearance before Senator Montoya's Special Hearings Committee on IRS Abuses, 1978,

- House Ways and Means Committee Appearance on New Tax Proposals, 1978,
- Staff Meeting, Joint Committee on Taxation-regarding Section 530 of the Revenue Act of 1978,
- Q Clearance-Atomic Energy Commission,
- Confidential Clearance Federal Bureau of Investigation,
- Marquis', Who's Who in the World and Who's Who in American Law,
- Michigan Assigned Appellate Counsel,
- Van Buren County, Michigan Court Appointed Defense Lawyer for indigents,
- Civil Mediator (Van Buren, Kalamazoo & Berrien Counties),
- Member, Mediation Committee Kalamazoo Bar Association,
- DePaul University Alumni Association High School Representative,
- Speaker, American College of Trial Lawyers (1997),
- Seminar Speaker, Independent Contractor Issue
- Computer and Internet skilled.

TEACHING EXPERIENCE
- Taught course in Torts for the American Institute for Paralegal Studies, Inc. (1989),
- Lectured on Poverty Law at DePaul University Law School.
- Adjunct Instructor, Political Science, Grand Rapids Community College (1999).

PAST EMPLOYMENT
- Assistant U.S. Attorney (Chicago-1971-1974),
- Staff Attorney, Argonne IL., National Laboratory (1968-1971),
- Supervisory Attorney, Montrose Legal Aid Bureau (Chicago-1966-1968),
- Attorney, Edwin F. Mandel Legal Aid Clinic of the University of Chicago Law School (1965-1966).

ACADEMIC PUBLICATIONS
- Casenote, "Real Property—Business Compulsion: Exaction of Overpayment", 12 DePaul Law Review 351 (1963),
- Comment, "Attorney-Client Privilege: Does it Apply to Corporations," 12 DePaul Law Review 263 (1963),
- Co-authored Articles Trial Magazine, "The Federal Preliminary Examination," ATLA (Spring, 1979) also appearing in Barrister and Law Notes of the American Bar Association,
- Lincoln Award, Illinois State Bar Association writing contest, "Conflict in Illinois Courts on Choice of Law Theory—Is It Lex Loci Delictus or Substantial Interest" (Nov., 1977 Illinois Bar Journal),
- Articles in Decalogue Journal, Vol. 24, No. 2 at p. 8 (Fall/Winter, 1976-77) "State Liability for Commission of Federal Civil Rights Violations by Its Employees" and Vol. 26 at p. 16 (Winter/Spring 1979-80) "Tax Complexity vs. Simplicity."

OTHER PUBLICATIONS
- Book Review, "Julian Jaynes, The Origin of Consciousness in The Breakdown of the Bicameral Mind," Vol. 434 Annals, American Academy of Political and Social Science, p. 239 (Nov. 1977),
- "In the Teeth of the Wind-A Study of Power and How to Fight It" (2002),
- Editor, "New Z Letter." (1980-81).

SAMPLE OF SOME NOTEWORTHY REPORTED CASES
- Marchlik v.Coronet Insurance Co., 239 N.E. 2d 299 (IL Supreme Court, 1968),
- Vitale v. INS., 463 F.2d 579 (7th Cir. 1972),
- Ramirez v. Weinberger, 365 F. Supp. 105 (3 Judge, N.D. IL. 1973) aff'd Per Curiam, 415 U.S., 970,

- U.S. v. Lomar Discount, Ltd., 61 F.R.D. 420 aff'd., 498 F.2d 1404 (7th Cir. 1974),
- U.S.v. Dema, 544 F. 2d 1373 (1976),
- U.S.ex. rel. Stewart v. Scott, 501 F.Supp. 53 (N.D. IL., 1980),
- Powe v. City of Chicago and County of Cook, 664 F.2d 639 (7th Cir. 1982),
- Dema v. Feddor, 470 F.Supp. 152 (N.D. IL. 1979) aff'd., 661 F.2d 936,
- Tabcor Sales Clearing, Inc. v. Department of Treasury, 471 F.Supp. 436 (N.D. IL., 1979),
- Illinois v. Gorman, 421 N.E. 2d 228 and 444 N.E. 2d 776 (1st District, IL. App. Ct., 1981 and 1982),
- Lipsey v.Chicago Cook County Criminal Justice Commission, 629 F.Supp. 955 (N.D. IL., 1986),
- Lipsey v. Illinois Human Rights Commission, 510 N.E. 2d 1226 (1st District, IL., App.Ct., 1987),
- Vogel v. Social Security Administration, 735 F.Supp.1353 (N.D. IL. 1989),
- Chief Trial Attorney, Michigan v. Fisher, 483 N.W. 2d 452 (Mi. App. Ct., 1992),
- Norwood Industries, Inc. v. Grand Blanc Printing, Inc., 556 N. W. 2d 897 (Mi. App. Ct., 1996).

ACTIVITIES
- Past Vice-President, South Haven Center for the Arts,
- Member Downer's Grove Architectural Commission,
- JAA Sponsor,
- Soccer Coach, Referee and Announcer.

HOBBIES
- Autograph and coin collecting, boating, golf, botany, history, trap shooting and hunting.

HISTORY OF PRACTICE
- Since 1975, I have been engaged in the sole practice of law, along with associates throughout the United States, who are consulted on a need basis. We have a boutique practice. Our emphasis has been on Major and Complex civil and criminal, state and federal litigation, Federal Tax and Constitutional litigation.

(Revised, 2003)

0-595-26272-4